Praise for Lead Like the Lord

"Kirk Brothers has blessed us with a rigorously biblical and thoroughly practical look at church leadership. His writing is fresh and filled to the brim with useful ideas you can put to work right away. More joy and effectiveness await those who 'lead like the Lord.'"

—Aubrey Johnson, Author of *Successful Shepherds*

"Dr. Kirk Brothers has written an outstanding book on leadership. His scholarship in this area is complemented by a wealth of experience in local churches, mission points, and Christian education. *Lead Like the Lord* strikes a healthy balance between theory and practice and will serve as a great resource for church leaders."

—Mark A. Blackwelder, Ph.D
Dean of the College of Biblical Studies
Freed-Hardeman University

"Dr. Kirk Brother's passion for following Jesus within the context of the church makes *Lead Like the Lord* unique. You will be challenged in your own walk of leadership as you read. You will enjoy the stories. You will be pointed to Scripture. Ultimately, you will love the example of Christ more because of spending time with Kirk as a guide along your journey."

—Michael Jackson, Ed.D
Co-Director
Heritage Christian Leadership Institute

"Powerful ... *Lead Like the Lord* will challenge you to become a more effective leader, not only in the church, but in all areas of your life. Kirk's discussions and insight will help you apply the leadership principles found in Jesus' own ministry."

—Dennis Stephen
Board Member, Heritage Christian University
Retired Chief Operating Officer, Life Operations
Farm Bureau Insurance of Tennessee

LEAD LIKE THE LORD

Lessons in Leadership from Jesus

W. KIRK BROTHERS

HERITAGE
CHRISTIAN UNIVERSITY
PRESS

Lead Like the Lord: Lessons in Leadership from Jesus

Published by Heritage Christian University Press

Copyright © 2021 by W. Kirk Brothers

Manufactured in the United States of America

Cataloging-in-Publication Data

Brothers, W. Kirk (Wilburn Kirk),

Lead like the Lord: lessons in leadership from Jesus / by W. Kirk Brothers

p. cm.

ISBN 978-1-7320483-8-6 (hbk.) 978-1-7347665-9-2 (ebook)

1. Christian leadership. 2. Jesus Christ. I. Author. II. Title.

253—dc20 LCCN: 2021907467

Scripture quotations are from the ESV® Bible (The Holy Bible, English Standard Version®), copyright © 2001 by Crossway, a publishing ministry of Good News Publishers. Used by permission. All rights reserved.

Scripture taken from the New King James Version®. Copyright © 1982 by Thomas Nelson. Used by permission. All rights reserved.

New American Standard Bible®, Copyright © 1960, 1971, 1977, 1995, 2020 by The Lockman Foundation. All rights reserved.

Cover design by Brittany Vander Maas.

For information:
Heritage Christian University Press
3625 Helton Drive
PO Box HCU
Florence, AL 35630
www.hcu.edu

Heritage Christian Leadership Institute

The Mission of the Heritage Christian Leadership Institute is to provide workshops, seminars, and resources that train godly servant-leaders who can serve as leaders in congregations, families, and communities with an emphasis on training elders and deacons.

A resource of the Heritage Christian Leadership Institute in cooperation with Heritage Christian University Press

Dedication

Cindy Markham Brothers
the strength in my knees, the compass in my head,
and the hope in my heart

Joe Brothers
the first leader I ever saw

Dorothy Brothers
the first person who believed in me

Preface

I grew up around leadership. My dad, Joe, has been a leader as long as I can remember: polyurethane belt development manager and later plant manager for the Gates Corporation; president of the Polyurethane Manufacturers Association; senior vice president of the National Management Association; chairman of the Kentucky State School Board; president of the Kentucky School Board Association; elder at three different congregations; and preacher of God's word. My mom, Dorothy, is leader builder and encourager. I also married a leader builder and encourager in my wife, Cindy. If my dad and I accomplish anything in our lives, it will be because of these two amazing and godly women! Cindy learned to be a leader builder from her mom, Louise Markham. Cindy's dad, Roy Markham, served first as a factory foreman and then later served many years as a Gospel preacher at various congregations across the south.

Because of organizations like Junior Achievement, opportunities given to me at Elizabethtown Independent

Schools, and congregations in Kentucky that would let me preach for them; I was able learn about leadership as a teenager through real-world experience. Preacher/Leadership training camps at the Pennington Bend church of Christ and Freed-Hardeman University gave me additional training in my high school years. After high school, I learned even more about leadership at the university level at Lipscomb University, Freed-Hardeman University, and Southern Seminary. So many professors impacted my understanding of leadership: Tom Holland, William Woodson, Marlin Connelly, Billy Smith, Earl Edwards, Hal Pettigrew, and Dennis Williams, to name a few.

God allowed me to work with wonderful churches in Elizabethtown, Kentucky; Hatley, Mississippi; McMinnville, Tennessee; Columbia, Tennessee; and Selmer, Tennessee. I worked with and under amazing leaders in these congregations who patiently shaped and molded me. I spent eight special years as a professor at Freed-Hardeman University. I saw leadership modeled by such people as Billy Smith, Dean of Bible; and Mark Blackwelder, Director of Graduate Studies. I served under two presidents, Joe Wiley and David Shannon. I learned much from these men that I use in my current position at Heritage Christian University. President Shannon and I have been friends since high school. He has also served on the board of Heritage Christian University. His encouragement has been a blessing to my life.

Since arriving at HCU, I have continued to learn from our board of trustees and from the wonderful leaders employed at the university (especially our administrative council). I was also able to participate in the Executive Training Program of the Association for Biblical Higher

Education (our accrediting agency). Throughout my life, starting with my parents, I have been encouraged and guided to be a student of God's word. It is in God's word that have learned the most powerful and life-transforming lessons on leadership. I believe with all of my heart that Jesus is the greatest leader to ever walk the earth and that the Bible is the greatest book on leadership.

Here is the point of all of this: This book is the outgrowth of a lifetime of people pouring their love and learning into my life, giving me opportunities to lead, and opening God's word to me. If you find anything helpful in this book, credit and thank them. Ultimately, this book is not about me sharing what I have learned. It is about challenging us to sit at the feet of Jesus and to learn to lead from Him. All Christians are to be shaped into the image of Christ (2 Corinthians 3:18). Jesus called His apostles to lead the way that He led (cf. John 13:12–16; Luke 22:24–27). Thus, the goal of this book is to challenge us to both live and lead like the Lord. I pray it hits its target.

In addition to the people and congregations listed above, there are others I wish to thank in relation to the publication of this book. First of all, I want to thank the capable and dedicated Heritage Christian University employees who labor tirelessly for Heritage Christian University Press: Bill Bagents, Brad McKinnon, and Jamie Cox. I am grateful to Brittany Vander Maas for the excellent cover artwork. I am deeply indebted to Melissa McFerrin for the numerous hours of editorial work she put in before the rough draft was ever sent to the Press Committee! (and even some work afterward). I thank Michael Jackson, Ed Gallagher, and Nathan Daily for editing specific portions of the book. I also appreciate Mark

Blackwelder, Michael Jackson, Aubrey Johnson, and Dennis Stephen for reviewing the book. Finally, I thank the advisory board of the Heritage Christian Leadership Institute for supporting the publication of this text: Boyd Pate, Don Snodgrass, Mark Miller, Dale Kirkland, Thomas Holiday, Jerry Kirk, Chuck Morris, and Marty Gray. Even though the people mentioned above participated in some way in the production of this book, it does not necessarily mean that they agree with every statement I make in the book.

Most of all, I thank our Lord, who not only teaches us how to lead but uses us in His service in spite of our brokenness! To Him be the glory!

Contents

LEAD LIKE THE LORD

LEARNING TO LEAD LIKE JESUS

Introduction

HUGO McCORD, a gospel preacher I knew since childhood, was correct when he noted, "A boy will not stumble as much when he puts his feet in his father's snow-tracks. So a preacher, when he steadily keeps his eyes on Jesus, will stumble less. One reason the Lord came into the world was to make tracks" (1996, 23). One goal of this book is to rekindle a deep respect for Jesus Christ in the heart of every Christian who reads it, and every leader in particular, that will inspire us to observe His life more intently, study His word more deeply, and imitate His example more precisely. Learning what made Jesus the greatest leader can help each of us do what we do more effectively. The characteristics that made Him a success can help one to be a better accountant, or sales manager, or mechanic, or farmer, or elder. Come; let us walk in His footsteps.

Why Look at Jesus?

Jesus had no formal training other than the training that any typical Jewish boy would receive growing up. He did not come from a family with wealth. He was described by John the immerser as "the Lamb of God" (John 1:29). Ironically, when His family went up to Jerusalem after His birth to offer sacrifices, they could not afford a lamb to sacrifice for the Lamb of God. Instead, they made the offering of two birds, the offering of the poor (Luke 2:22–24; cf. Lev. 12:8). He also had no political or military might. He did not have an army with swords, shields, and horses behind Him. He held no high office. He did not grow up in a palace. Jesus was a simple peasant. He grew up as a carpenter in a community that was looked down on by many. Due to the nature of His birth (by the power of the Holy Spirit), there would have been those who would have questioned the integrity of His mother and father.

Yet, He changed the world. His apostles traversed the Roman Empire to tell the world about Him, even though it meant death for most of them. Billions have been impacted by His life. Millions have become His followers. Countless committed disciples have marched into the arena to face the lions in His name or have boldly proclaimed their faith in Him while bound to a stake as the flames leapt up around them. Two thousand years after His death, He is known by people spanning the globe. The book that tells His story is the bestselling book of all time. I am reminded of John 6. Many disciples were leaving Jesus. They were merely curious followers, not committed ones. Jesus turned to the apostles and said, "Do you want to go away as well?" (6:67). Peter's response is one of the most powerful statements in Scripture: "Lord, to whom shall we go? You have the words of eternal life" (6:68). I think Peter's statement could also apply to our study of spiritual leadership: "Lord, to whom shall we go?" Whom could we consider that would be better than the most influential person to ever grace this planet?

The journey to this book began when I was in graduate school. My PhD work focused on leadership, and biblical leadership in particular. I read countless books and articles about leadership, I listened to professors who shared their knowledge and experience, I poured over page after page of research, and I typed hundreds of pages on the topic. One thing stood out to me repeatedly as I examined the research and literature on this topic. I kept noticing that many of the characteristics and habits of great leaders, which are being promoted in modern books and seminars and are revealed in modern research projects, were demonstrated by Jesus 2,000 years ago. For example, research drawn from over 200,000 people who rated over 25,000 leaders is highlighted in John H. Zenger and Joseph Folkman's book *The Extraordinary Leader*. They identified the following characteristics: "Leading Organizational Change," "Interpersonal Skills," "Personal Capability," "Focus on Results," and "Character" (2002, 13). In their monumental work *The Leadership Challenge,* James M. Kouzes and Barry Z. Posner explored the findings of their own research. They discovered five practices of exemplary leadership: "Model the Way," "Inspire a Shared Vision," "Challenge the Process," "Enable Others to Act," and "Encourage the Heart" (2017, 12–13). They also identified four primary characteristics that people look for and admire in their leaders: "Honest," "Competent," "Inspiring," and

"Forward-looking" (2017, 31). I believe you will find, as we study the ministry of Jesus, these characteristics being lived out in His life.

I will quote numerous leadership books throughout this book. So many quotes may cause you to feel, at times, like you are reading a term paper for a graduate class. There is a method to my madness. I have two primary reasons for doing this: (1) To identify books you might want to read for further study, and (2) to illustrate the reality that the principles that are often recommended today were taught and lived out by the Son of God long before we drew our first breaths.

Are We Ready to Learn from Jesus?

Professor of education Findley B. Edge, in his book titled *Teaching for Results*, notes the role of the student in the learning process: "The teacher is not the only one in the teaching-learning situation who causes action, reaction, and interaction. Some of these factors find their source in the learner" (1999, 37). We have established the fact that Jesus can teach us how to be great leaders, but we will learn little if we are not ready to be good listeners and learners.

Jesus stepped into a boat along the shore of the sea of Galilee and told one of the most popular and well known of all His parables, the parable of the soils.

> And when a great crowd was gathering and people from town after town came to him, he said in a parable, "A sower went out to sow his seed. And as he sowed, some fell along the path and was trampled underfoot, and the birds of the air devoured it. And some fell on the rock,

and as it grew up, it withered away, because it had no moisture. And some fell among thorns, and the thorns grew up with it and choked it. And some fell into good soil and grew and yielded a hundredfold." As he said these things, he called out, "He who has ears to hear, let him hear." (Luke 8:4–8, cf. Luke 8:9–15; Matt. 13:3–23; Mark 4:2–20)

Before proceeding with the meaning of the parable, let's talk a little bit about the cultural setting behind the parable. Craig S. Keener makes an important observation: "Most of the Roman Empire's inhabitants were rural peasant farmers or herders. The literate elite often ignored this large population, but Jesus's illustrations show that he ministered frequently among this class. Although Galilee was heavily populated with villages and boasted two major cities (Sepphoris and Tiberias), most of its inhabitants were rural, agrarian peasants" (1993, 82). Jesus spoke the cultural language of His audience. This is an important trait of leaders. Jesus's audience understood the agriculture behind the parable, but we may not. Our society is becoming less rural and less agricultural in orientation and more urban and technological.

My father grew up on a corn and cotton farm in Unionville, Tennessee. His family used mules, a pony, and a Farmall tractor for the farm work. They also did a great deal of work by hand (harvesting, for example). Farming is largely done by machinery today. In Jesus's day, seed was cast by hand, or it was allowed to trickle through holes in a sack (often carried by an animal). Sometimes the ground was plowed first; sometimes it wasn't. Thus, crops did not necessarily grow in a clearly defined area like they do on

5

many farms today. There were also many walking paths that traversed the landscape between houses and farms. Land in first century Judea tended to have a thin layer of soil with rock underneath. This reminds me of the soil of Bedford Country, Tennessee, where my dad grew up. The family farm was filled with large limestone rocks. Most of these rocks were covered by a layer of topsoil. As a result, you did not always know how deep the soil was. Thistles were a common problem on farms in Judea as well. Some were present when the seed was sown (if the field was not cleared and plowed). Even if the thistles were removed, it is likely that they were not pulled up by the roots but were simply cut off above ground and burned. This would allow the weeds to grow back and become a threat to the productive plants (cf. Keener 1993, 82). Harvests could range from 10 to 100 times the seeds planted in the fertile Jordan valley, but for most of the region of Judea the average return was tenfold (Keener 1993, 144).

Jesus often told parables without giving an explanation. Yet, in the case of the parable of the soils, He gave an explanation in response to a request from His disciples. He identified the four soils discussed in the parable: "road," "rocky," "thorny," and "good" soils. The "road" soil fell on the pathway. When a section of earth has been walked on enough, it can become as hard as concrete. I was reminded of this when I was doing archeological work at the ancient city of Caesarea. You could tell when your digging brought you to the dirt floor of an ancient home. It was much harder than the soil around it. It was like digging through concrete. Seeds cannot penetrate hard soil. Likewise, some hearts just will not listen.

Another soil was the "rocky" soil. This is the soil that

looks fertile, but there is a layer of rock a few inches under the surface (like parts of my grandparents' farm). The result is that the ground does not hold much water, and it quickly dries up in the dry season. Also, the shallow soil prevents the roots from digging deeply into the ground. Thus, the plant is weak and susceptible to extremes of weather. This soil illustrates the weak spiritual heart or temporary faith that starts with a bang, and then quits when trouble comes.

Next, Jesus noted the "thorny" soil. The thorns grow up around the good plants, drawing resources from the young plants and starving them to death. I am reminded of the early attempts by my wife and me to grow a garden. We would start well, and the garden would progress until all my summer traveling started. We would then get behind in tending the garden, and the weeds would take over. This illustrates the heart that is open to Jesus but is never able to let go of this world and this life. It is consumed with earthly things, and they choke out the heavenly things.

Finally, Jesus revealed the "good" soil. This soil produces a wonderful crop. It is soft and deep, rich with nutrients, and free of weeds. Jesus said that, spiritually speaking, this is the heart that is honest and good, holds tight to the word, bears fruit, and does not quit. You might be wondering why we would take the time to look at this parable. Why not just dive into the characteristics of the leadership of Jesus?

The answer to the question above is found in this statement by Jesus: "Take care then how you hear" (Luke 8:18). We will never learn to lead from and like Jesus unless our hearts are right. Therefore, we need to take some spiritual soil samples.

- Road Soil – Spiritual leaders are willing to learn. Am I?
- Rocky Soil – Spiritual leaders have strong faith and finish what they start. Will I?
- Thorny Soil – Spiritual leaders put heavenly things before earthly things. Do I?
- Good Soil – Spiritual leaders have humble and open hearts that listen and learn. Do I?

Do not continue with this book if you do not have a heart that is willing to accept the teachings and examples of Jesus and to put them into practice. Let us not be like the shallow disciples of John 6 who walked away. On the other hand, notice that Matthew 13:8 says the good soil produced thirtyfold, sixtyfold, and a hundredfold. This means that in some cases the harvest was one hundred times more than the amount planted. That is an incredible return on one's investment. If you told someone who plays the stock market that they would receive one hundred times what they invested, they would make a mad dash for a broker. The text is saying if we will honestly and humbly open ourselves up to learning from the words of Jesus, God can produce great things with our lives.

Conclusion

What are we trying to accomplish in this book? What are we aiming at? Every story needs a lead character, a ship needs a captain, and an arrow needs a target. Our lead, captain, and target for this book is Jesus, the Son of God. Each chapter in this book will begin by examining a characteristic of the leadership of the Christ and will then challenge Christians today to apply the lessons learned to their lives. We will use the letter "C" as our memory glue throughout this study, as we consider nine characteristics that made Jesus the greatest leader ever to walk the face of the earth. He was centered, connected, compassionate, common, clear thinking, competent, courageously calm, a coach, and a person of character. There are additional characteristics that might have been included. I pray that the ones I have chosen will whet your appetite for a lifelong study of learning to lead like the Lord. Jesus is the Son of God, so naturally there are things about His leadership that we can never emulate. Yet, I firmly believe that if we will seek to apply these nine principles, we can have an influence on others that will impact eternity.

Discussion Questions

1. What are some New Testament examples of the leadership ability of Jesus?
2. What is the best book you have every read on the subject of leadership (outside of the Bible)?
3. Can you name some principles in that book that are seen in the life of Jesus? If so, name some.
4. Name some examples in the Bible of the different types of soils mentioned in Jesus's parable.

Homework

1. Make a list of potential excuses that might keep you from completing this study.

2. Make a list of potential excuses that might keep you from putting the example of Jesus into action.

3. Consider what you will do to make sure those excuses do not stop you.

WHAT IS SPIRITUAL LEADERSHIP?

Introduction

You're twenty years old. You have your whole life ahead of you, but you are not sure how long that will last. Your home, family, car, and dreams are thousands of miles away. Today, you are in Afghanistan. You are part of a small patrol that is to infiltrate a small village along the Afghanistan/Pakistan border. Intel has reported a Taliban presence, and the responsibility of your eight-person patrol is to confirm or deny this intelligence. You have been on patrol before, but today is different. Today, the patrol leader has asked you to be the point man. It is your responsibility to go in first. You must see the enemy before he sees you. The lives of the seven soldiers behind you are in your hands. If you fail, they may die.

Your senses are on edge as you approach the outskirts of the village. You walk the dusty streets with one eye to the ground, looking for Improvised Explosive Devices (IEDs), and the other to the rooftops and windows, looking for snipers prepared to fire upon your patrol. You wonder if they can see you at this very moment.

Then, the silence is broken by the sound of gunfire. Bullets fly through the air and thud into the ground or splatter the mudbrick of buildings lining the street. You hear the grunts and screams of men around you as they are struck by flying lead. At least one man is down to your left. Another has been wounded. You look to your right and see that the family of the patrol leader is now without a father. As the shock of this reality hits you, a bullet does as well. It strikes your leg and sends you to your knees.

Thoughts go rushing through your mind. *Where are they? Will I lose my leg? Will I die? What do we do?* The radio operator comes up behind you and seeks advice. Though you are only twenty years old, you are the most experienced man left in the patrol. The surviving members of the patrol are looking to you. You must lead. You must assess the situation, devise a plan, and carry it out almost flawlessly, or none of you are going home. It is time to step up. It is time to lead. You are the point man! (Adapted from Farrar 1990, 14–16.)

Even if it is not taking place in war-torn Afghanistan, it is not easy being a leader. Bad things happen in families, businesses, churches, and countries where no one is willing to lead or where the leaders who step forward are not what they should be. The goal of this book is not only to challenge you to be a leader but to challenge you to lead like the Lord.

The Need for Leaders

Former University of Southern California professor and leadership author Warren Bennis states,

> Leadership is a word on everyone's lips. The young attack it, and the old grow wistful for it. Parents have lost it and police seek it. Experts claim it and artists spurn it, while scholars want it. Philosophers reconcile it (as authority) with liberty and theologians demonstrate its compatibility with conscience. If bureaucrats pretend they have it, politicians wish they did. Everyone agrees that there is less of it than there used to be (Bennis and Nanus 1985, 1).

We begin our study of the leadership of Jesus by wrestling with the shortage of capable leaders. Consider the quotes in the following paragraphs. They come from leadership experts in a variety of settings.

University of Michigan professor and author Noel M. Tichy highlights the need for leadership in the corporate world but broadens his comments to other arenas:

> The tank is low; we are not producing enough leaders at all levels, especially at the senior and CEO levels. Just consider the blue-chip companies that in the past decade have had to find outside candidates to replace their departing CEOs. ... This is a terrible track record when you consider that perhaps the No. 1 responsibility of a CEO is to develop other leaders who can carry on the legacy of the organization. Our leadership pipelines are broken. And this is also true in politics, diplomacy and

religious and social organizations as well as in business. (2002, xxii–xxiii)

EBay director Thomas Tierney notes the need for leadership in nonprofit circles:

> America's nonprofit sector, already expansive, is expanding. Most of us both contribute to the sector and benefit from it: we strengthen our communities when we give time and money to nonprofit organizations. Yet few of us are aware that those organizations face an insidious crisis that could undermine all their good works—a shortage of nonprofit leaders (2006, 95).

Tierney is cofounder of The Bridgespan Group. This is a nonprofit organization that provides consulting for philanthropists and nonprofits. Whether for-profit or nonprofit, the common message is that we need more quality leaders.

Now let us move to the religious arena. George Barna is known for his research on the Christian world at large. As he summarizes his findings, he states,

> The central conclusion is that the American church is dying due to a lack of strong leadership. In this time of unprecedented opportunity and plentiful resources, the church is actually losing influence. The primary reason is the lack of leadership (1997, 18).

J. J. Turner has been one of the key players in the area of leadership in the churches of Christ for many years. He has written countless books and conducted numerous seminars on the subject. He notes,

That the church is in a crisis mode relative to leaders and leadership, there should be little doubt; especially by those who monitor the state of leadership or try to enlist persons to serve in leadership roles. There are fewer and fewer volunteers to step up to the plate to lead or avail themselves of leadership training. Few, if any, churches are growing leaders, which is far more needed and challenging than merely training leaders (Turner 2013, 19).

Barna and Turner saw the same conditions in the religious world that Tichy and Tierney saw in the business sector. They each seem to agree with Bennis's assessment that when it comes to leadership, "there is less of it than there used to be" (Bennis and Nanus 1985, 1).

I have been working with churches on a regular basis since I was in high school. I have served as a preacher, youth minister, college minister, and deacon. I have searched for mentors for college and high school students. I have walked with several congregations through the process of appointing elders and deacons. I have witnessed the challenge to find men willing and able to step into these positions. I have felt the struggle to find classroom leaders when I served as a deacon of education. I have also been part of the search process for leaders in various positions at two Christian schools. The point is that my personal experience is consistent with what the authors above are saying. We need more leaders.

The Definition of Leadership

While it seems obvious to this writer that we need leaders, it seems equally obvious that we need the right kind of leaders. That is the heart of this book. We do not just want leaders; we want leaders who lead like the Lord. Before we wrestle with the kind of leaders we need to be, we need to consider what leadership is. The kind of person an employer looks for when hiring depends a great deal on the job the potential employee is being hired for. What then is the "job" of a leader? What is leadership?

Defining Leadership

Joseph C. Rost laments the fact that there is no single, common definition of leadership that is used by all (1993, 99). He then, of course, proposes his own definition as "the" definition. (We will note his definition below.) While his definition is very helpful, I am not prepared to say it is the one that all should use. I also do not presume that my definition of leadership should be "the" definition of leadership. Still, I will share it below because I want you to know the perspective on leadership that I come from as I write this book. Let us look at some of the definitions of leadership that are out there:

- "At its most basic, leadership is influence" (Ogden and Meyer 2007, 9).
- "Leadership is influence—nothing more, nothing less" (Maxwell 2007, vi).
- "Leadership is an influence relationship among leaders and followers who intend real changes

that reflect their mutual purposes" (Rost 1993, 102).

- "To put it simply, leadership is *influence*. The ideal leader is someone whose life and character motivate people to follow. ... Leadership is not about style or technique as much as it is about character" (MacArthur 2004, vi–vii).
- "Leadership is the art and practice of exerting an influence on the behavior and beliefs of others. Leaders shape and influence people, institutions, and events" (Sloan 2011, 8).
- "Leadership is the lifting of a man's vision to higher sights, the raising of a man's performance to a higher standard, the building of a man's personality beyond its normal limitations" (Drucker 1974, 463).
- "Leadership is a process ordinary people use when they are bringing forth the best from themselves and others" (Kouzes and Posner 2004, 2).
- "Leadership is mobilizing others toward a goal shared by the leader and followers" (Garry Wills qtd. in Barna 1997, 21).
- "In sum, then, leadership involves a person, group, or organization who shows the way in an area of life—whether in the short- or the long-term—and in doing so both influences and empowers enough people to bring about change in that area" (Banks and Ledbetter 2004, 16–17).
- "Leaders are people movers." (David Shannon, President of Freed-Hardeman University, in a

statement made in lesson at a leadership
workshop in Tennessee).

Note some things these definitions have in common.
Notice, in particular, the repetition of "influence" and its
synonyms and terms like "mutual purposes" and "goals."
As you reflect on these definitions, let me share mine with
you: "Leadership is the act of guiding or influencing the
attitudes and/or actions of others toward a goal or set of
goals." You do not have to agree with this definition, but at
least you will know where I am coming from.

Defining Spiritual Leadership

Now let us focus on a specific type of leadership, spiritual
leadership. Seminary president Albert Mohler states,

> I believe that leadership is all about putting the right
> beliefs into action, and knowing, on the basis of
> convictions, what those right beliefs and actions are. This
> book is written with the concern that far too much of
> what passes for leadership today is mere management.
> Without convictions you might be able to manage, but
> you cannot really lead (2012, 26).

In other words, leadership is not just about moving
people somewhere; it is moving them in the right direction
based on the right convictions. For spiritual leaders, Mohler
would emphasize that these convictions must be based on
biblical truth.

In *Christian Leadership Essentials*, edited by David Dockery,
university president Robert Sloan states, "Leaders shape

and influence people, institutions, and events. Leaders and leadership are determined not by the number of followers but by the changes effected over time for the good of God's world" (2011, 8). I like the emphasis that Sloan puts on the fact that leaders often bring about change. He also says that these changes are for "the good of God's world." This is consistent with what my friend Aubrey Johnson says about leadership: "Doing good to others is the trademark of true leadership and genuine greatness" (Johnson 2014, 2). Spiritual leaders lead toward goals that are good for God's world and God's church. Our goals should be God's goals.

Dr. Michael S. Wilder was one of my professors in my doctoral program. He wrote a book with one of his fellow professors, Dr. Timothy Paul Jones, whom I have also been able to hear on several occasions. Here is their definition of the Christian leader's function and purpose:

> The Christ-following leader—living as a bearer of God's image in union with Christ and his people—develops a diverse community of fellow laborers who are equipped and empowered to pursue shared goals that fulfill the creation mandate and the Great Commission in submission to the Word of God (Wilder and Jones 2018, 16).

Notice the emphasis on "goals" that we saw in the earlier definitions. I appreciate several aspects of Wilder and Jones's definition, but in particular the ideas of being a bearer of God's image, following Christ, and submitting to God's word.

Greg Ogden and Daniel Meyer offer helpful insight into spiritual leadership when they say, "Christian leadership is

Christlike influence" (2007, 9). Many of the definitions noted above stress that leadership is about influence. Ogden and Meyer are stressing that spiritual leaders influence others by emulating and being influenced themselves by Jesus. This is consistent with the emphasis in the definition by Wilder and Jones. The book you are reading is written based on the belief that it is Jesus who teaches us how to influence others the way God wants us to.

One of my favorite definitions of leadership comes from one of my former graduate school professors, Dr. Kenneth O. Gangel. Dr. Gangel defines spiritual leadership as "the exercise of one's spiritual gifts under the call of God to serve a certain group of people in achieving the goals God has given them toward the end of glorifying Christ" (Gangel 1997, 44). Notice, again, the stress on moving toward God's goals. Observe his emphasis on the fact that when leaders use gifts from God, they are in some sense answering a call from God, and the goal is to glorify Christ (not the leader). This is powerful.

With the above in mind, here is my definition of spiritual leadership in particular: "Spiritual leadership describes the actions of a servant leader who follows God's example and uses God's gifts to guide people toward God's goals for God's glory." There are some things I want you to notice in my definition.

- "Actions" – Leadership is about doing something, not just having power.
- "Servant-leader" – Spiritual leaders lead for the benefit of the led.
- "God's example" – God shows us how to be leaders; integrity is important.

- "God's gifts" – Leadership ability is from God (whether given through biological, experiential, or educational means).
- "Guide people" – Leaders are influencers, "people movers" (cf. Shannon).
- "God's goals" – If we are spiritual leaders, the goals should be God's, not ours.
- "God's glory" – The purpose of the church is to glorify God (Eph. 3:21); leaders in the church should seek the same.

The definition above gives you my basic philosophy of leadership. It will resurface from time to time as we move through this study.

Conclusion

I like to whittle. I start with a chunk of wood, envision the spoon or butter knife that might be in the wood, and carve away what is not a spoon or knife. The process starts with a chunk of wood. My definition of spiritual leadership does not have to be your definition, but it may be able to serve as a chunk of spiritual wood that you can use to envision and carve your own definition of leadership. Remember that definition determines doing. How we define leadership will determine how we do leadership.

Discussion Questions

1. From your personal experience, do you believe

there are leadership problems in our cultures
and churches? Share some examples.

2. Was there a definition of leadership in this
chapter that you most agreed with? Why or
why not?

3. What is your personal definition of leadership?

4. What is your personal definition of spiritual
leadership?

5. How, if any, did your definition of leadership
change as a result of this chapter?

Homework

1. Interview several leaders you know and ask
them for their definition of leadership and/or
spiritual leadership.

2. Work together with others in your congregation
or organization to develop a common definition
of leadership that can guide your actions and
decisions.

3

CENTERED

HE UNDERSTOOD HIS PURPOSE

Introduction

ONE OF MY favorite stories concerns a man who was driving into a small town and noticed something strange. There were targets everywhere, you know, the kind you aim at with a gun or bow and arrow. They were painted on tree trunks, the sides of buildings, and on wooden park benches. What was also interesting was that there was an arrow in the middle of the bull's eye on every target. This was amazing to the stranger driving into the town. As he approached the town square, he noticed a man walking on the sidewalk. His curiosity compelled him to pull over, lower his window, and ask the man on the sidewalk a question. "Who is this amazing archer you have in your town?" The man had a puzzled look on his face and responded, "What amazing archer?" The driver then observed, "Someone put an arrow in the bull's eye of all of these targets, so you must have an amazing archer!" With a snicker, the man on the sidewalk responded, "We do not have an archer; we have an artist. He randomly shoots arrows and then paints targets around them" (adapted from Cohen and Stewart 1994, 219). I love that story because, to me, it illustrates how many of us live our lives. We do not wake up each day aiming at something. We just stay busy all day and count where we ended up as the bull's eye. Success often comes to those with a sense of purpose and a mental vision of what that purpose looks like when lived out. There are just some people who have a sense of where they are going. They are not wandering aimlessly through life. They are going somewhere. They are aiming at something. They are spiritual archers. Jesus was such a person.

With this chapter, we begin our focus on characteristics of the leadership of Jesus. We begin by noticing that He lived a "centered" life. Jesus came to earth with a very clear purpose before Him. Many people misunderstood His focus, some tried to stop Him from fulfilling His purpose, and others tried to change His purpose. In spite of these obstacles, Jesus was firmly "centered" on what He came to earth to do.

The Christ

There has been a great deal of emphasis in the last twenty years or so on being "purpose-driven." Books like *The Purpose Driven Life*, *The Purpose Driven Church*, and *Purpose Driven Youth Ministry* have leapt off the shelves. If there was ever a life driven by purpose, it was the life of Jesus Christ. In his book, *Visioneering*, Andy Stanley states,

A *clear* vision, along with the courage to follow through, dramatically increases your chances of coming to end of your life, looking back with a deep abiding satisfaction, and thinking, *I did it. I succeeded. I finished well. My life counted.* Without a clear vision, odds are you will come to the end of your life and wonder. Wonder what you could have done—what you should have done (2016, 8–9).

Jesus finished well. In fact, some of His last words were, "It is finished!" (John 19:30, cf. John 17:4). You cannot finish something if you do not have a goal of something to accomplish in the first place.

A Person on Purpose

One begins to see early on in the Gospels that Jesus had a higher calling. His very name was a reminder of His purpose. Notice what the angel of the Lord said to Joseph in Matthew's Gospel: "She will bear a son; and you shall call his name Jesus, for he will save his people from their sins" (Matt. 1:21). Jesus's name in Greek was *Iēsoûs*. This was the Greek form of His Hebrew name, *Yeshua* (i.e., Joshua). His name means "Yahweh saves" (Rogers and Rogers 1998, 2) or "Yahweh is salvation" (Hagner 1993, 19). The angel said He was to be given this name because "he will save his people from their sins" (Matt. 1:21). He was to be God's (Yahweh's) means of saving the world. Every time someone said Jesus's name, they were proclaiming His purpose. I am reminded of the words of Peter in Acts 4: "And is there salvation in no one else, for there is no other name under heaven given among men by which we must be saved" (Acts 4:12).

There is a powerful moment recorded in the Gospel of Luke that tells of Jesus embracing His life's "higher calling."

While sitting in the temple in Jerusalem and conversing with the religious scholars, a twelve-year-old Jesus said to His parents, "Why were you looking for me? Did you not know that I must be in my Father's house?" (Luke 2:49). The New King James Version translates the end of this verse as "about My Father's business." The text literally says something along the lines of "to be in the *things* of my father" (*eînai en toîs toû patrós mou*; these transliterated Greek words are reordered here to better fit English word flow). The words "business," "house," and "things" are not actually in the text. There is only the article ("the") with an implied noun to follow. Translators must decide if "things" (or the implied noun) refers to the place where they are (i.e., "temple/house") or the things which are important to God ("business").

Either way one translates this phrase, the point is the same. Jesus was embracing His purpose. Jesus played off the word "father." His mother had just said, "Behold, your father and I have been searching for you in great distress" (Luke 2:48). Mary was talking about Joseph when she referenced "your father." In Jesus's response He was referring to a different father, His heavenly Father. Jesus understood that His life's purpose came from the Father above. He knew He was here on earth to focus on God's things. Over eighteen years later, Jesus was still faithful to this mission. In John 6:38 He states, "For I have come down from heaven, not to do my own will, but the will of him who sent me." Jesus's life was a life lived on purpose. When we board a plane or cruise ship, we want to know that the pilot knows where he or she is going and how to get there. People followed Jesus because He was "centered." He knew where He was going and how to get there.

A Person with Priorities

Jesus made a number of statements in the Gospels concerning why He came. You might take a moment to read the "I have come" statements in the Gospel of John, for example (cf. John 5:43; 6:38; 7:28; 10:10; 12:27, 46; 18:37). All His statements would fall under the umbrella purpose of carrying out His Father's business. I would like to focus on three goals or priorities that Jesus focused on within His overall mission: "Portraying God," "Proclaiming God's Kingdom," and "Providing Salvation on the Cross."

Portraying God

In John 5, Jesus stated, "I have come in my Father's name" (John 5:43). He came to earth as the Father's representative. This included not only fulfilling the Father's mission but also showing humanity the Father's nature. The words of John 1:18 embody this reality: "No one has ever seen God; the only God, who is at the Father's side, he has made him known." Jesus could do this because "He is the image of the invisible God" (Col. 1:15) and "the exact imprint of his nature" (Heb. 1:3). Through His miracles we see God's power. Through His love we see God's grace. This is why Jesus could say to Philip, the apostle, "Whoever has seen me has seen the Father" (John 14:9).

Proclaiming the Kingdom

Jesus came to show us the Father. He also came to preach. Luke 4 gives us a picture of Jesus, the local carpenter, coming back to His home synagogue congregation on a sabbath. He was asked to be one of the Scripture readers for the day. The congregational keeper of the scrolls handed him the scroll of the book of Isaiah. Jesus opened it to what would be Isaiah 61 in our Bibles and read,

> The Spirit of the Lord is upon me, because he has anointed me to proclaim good news to the poor. He has sent me to proclaim liberty to the captives and recovering of sight to the blind, to set at liberty those who are oppressed, to proclaim the year of the Lord's favor (Luke 4:18–19).

This passage from Isaiah was commonly believed by first-century Jews to be a reference to the Messiah. After reading the Messianic passage, Jesus said, "Today this Scripture has been fulfilled in your hearing" (Luke 4:21). That was one of Jesus's "drop the mic" moments. He was declaring that He is the Messiah. He was also declaring that preaching was part of His mission.

Luke 7 finds John the immerser in prison. This is likely not where John envisioned his ministry leading. He seems to have wanted to make sure that he had led people to the correct Messiah. He sent his disciples to ask Jesus, "Are you the one who is to come, or shall we look for another?" (Luke 7:20). Jesus did not immediately answer their question. Instead, He began to perform miracles in their presence and then stated, "Go and tell John what you have seen and heard: the blind receive their sight, the lame walk, lepers are cleansed, and the deaf hear, the dead are raised up, the poor have good news preached to them" (Luke 7:22). Notice that Jesus referred to elements of the quote from Isaiah 61 that He read in the synagogue in chapter 4.

His proof that He was the Messiah was that He did what the Messiah was supposed to do. This included preaching the good news.

Providing Salvation on the Cross

Peter summarized what the Father's plan was for Jesus's earthly life and death: "The God of our fathers raised Jesus, whom you killed by hanging him on a tree. God exalted him at his right hand as Leader and Savior, to give repentance to Israel and forgiveness of sins" (Acts 5:30–31). Did you notice the words "Leader and Savior"? This book is about His leadership. However, we need to be reminded that His leadership included dying on a cross. Jesus came so that "all flesh shall see the salvation of God" (Luke 3:6). Jesus worded it this way: "For the Son of Man came to seek and to save the lost" (Luke 19:10; cf. Luke 5:31–32). A simple journey through the Gospel of Mark reveals that Jesus was on a mission (cf. Mark 8:31–33; 9:31–32; 10:32–34). His entire life pointed toward Jerusalem and the cross. Jesus was not here on earth just to enjoy the scenery. He was here with a purpose. He came to die in order that He might provide salvation for all humanity. When Peter rebuked Jesus (Can you imagine that?) for talking about dying, Jesus responded, "Get behind me, Satan!" (Mark 8:33). This is almost exactly the same thing Jesus said to Satan himself in Matthew 4:10. In that moment, Peter was doing Satan's bidding. Jesus would let no one divert Him from carrying out His purpose, not even His closest followers and friends.

Prioritizing His Goals

Jesus carried out the Father's will through the three goals listed above. These three goals did not all have equal value. For example, Jesus showed people the Father and that He was from the Father through the performing of miracles. An example of this can be seen in Luke 4:31–41. Jesus spent a Sabbath day in Capernaum teaching, healing, and casting out demons. The next day Jesus went to a deserted place to be alone with God. The crowds came looking for Him. They likely wanted more healings or demons cast out. There would have been many other people who needed to be healed. Jesus's answer is insightful: "I must preach the good news of the kingdom of God to the other towns as well, for I was sent for this purpose" (Luke 4:43). While Jesus wanted to help as many people as possible with their physical needs, He knew that it was more important that He help them with their spiritual needs. If He stayed to heal the people in Capernaum, then there were people in other villages who would not hear the message of salvation. Jesus prioritized proclaiming the Kingdom over miraculously rescuing people from pain and poverty. Ultimately, the highest priority for Jesus was providing salvation on the cross. When did Jesus stop preaching? He stopped when they put Him on trial (cf. Mark 14:61). The one man who had confounded countless opponents with His wisdom and teaching, who could have been His own defense attorney, chose, for the most part, to remain silent during His trial. Why? Because His mission was not to win in court but to die on a cross and win over sin.

The Christian

Jesus left us a pattern to practice. Christian leaders also need a sense of purpose. Author David Fisher notes that preachers are becoming an endangered species because they lack a sense of identity. So many things are expected of them that they struggle to narrow their focus and answer the question, "Who am I?" (1996, 24). Preachers are not the only ones who struggle with finding their true purpose. It can happen to any Christian and any Christian leader. We often fail because we have no sense of identity. Fisher states, "God wants us to know that our primary cues come from him. Our identity is found in his Son, who calls us to his service. ... Our sense of purpose and success must come from our identity as Christ's servants" (1996, 28). If we are truly servants of Christ, focusing on Jesus's purpose helps us find our purpose.

A People on Purpose

Let us return to my definition of spiritual leadership: "Spiritual leadership describes the actions of a servant leader who follows God's example and uses God's gifts *to guide people toward God's goals* for God's glory." Spiritual leaders should not just hold a position; they should be taking people somewhere. They should be guiding or influencing people to move in the direction God wants them to move in. What are God's goals? The purpose and goals of Jesus can help us answer that question. Jesus helped people to know God, told people the good news of God's Kingdom, and made a way for people to be saved. Since the church is the body of Christ (Eph. 1:22–23), shouldn't the mission of the church be to continue the work of Jesus? I understand that only Jesus can die for people's sins, but the church can and should continue Jesus's work of seeking and saving the lost (cf. Luke 19:10). Leaders need to keep focused on the purpose of the church as they make decisions and lead God's people.

A Personal Purpose (Individual and Congregational Mission Statements)

I am a big believer in mission statements. This belief was influenced by Stephen R. Covey's monumental work, *The Seven Habits of Highly Effective People*. Habit number two, for Covey, was "begin with the end in mind." Covey stated, "To begin with the end in mind means to start with a clear understanding of your destination" (1989, 98). He adds that this principle "is based on the principle that *all things are created twice*" (1989, 99). The first creation is in the mind, and the second creation is in the physical world. The vision in our heads will become the realities created by our hands.

Covey encouraged leaders to develop a personal mission statement. I followed his advice many years ago, and it has served me well. I have served in two universities which had clear mission statements. I helped to design the mission statement for the youth and family ministry program at one of these schools. I have worked with leadership to craft a mission statement and list of goals for two different congregations. Here are some various mission statements that may help you to think about what you might do.

- My personal mission statement: "The goal of

my life is to model and proclaim the good news
of Jesus Christ to my family, my local
congregation, the Lord's church at large, my
community, my country, and the world such that
it will motivate conversion to Christ, maturity
into the likeness of Christ, and ministry as an
active part of the body of Christ."

- Graymere church of Christ mission statement:
"To know Him, to share Him, to live with Him
in heaven. We long to know God more deeply,
to share His love and salvation with the world,
and to dwell in His presence for eternity. Our
mission is embodied in four words:

Magnify - We seek to praise God in
spirit and truth (John 4:24).

Minister - We each seek to find a place to
minister in His Kingdom (Eph. 4:12).

Mature - We seek to grow daily into
the likeness of Christ (Eph. 4:13).

Mission - We seek, as His body, to make
Christ's mission our mission (Eph. 1:22–23;
Luke 4:18–19).

To portray God's love
To proclaim God's Kingdom
To provide salvation to the lost
The word of God is our guiding light as we
endeavor to realize this mission."
(Psalms 119:105).

- Heritage Christian University mission
statement: "Heritage Christian University exists
for the advancement of churches of Christ by
equipping servants through undergraduate and

graduate programs and continuing education. HCU produces effective communicators, preachers, teachers and missionaries for real-world ministry with a focus on evangelism and a commitment to Scripture."

- Freed-Hardeman University youth and family ministry program mission statement: "The Bachelor of Arts in youth and family ministry is designed to provide majors with a core of courses that will prepare them for the role of a youth minister in the church with emphasis on training them to teach God's word to adolescents and assisting parents in raising their children to accept Christ, mature into the likeness of Christ, and minister in the name of Christ."

I encourage every individual, congregation, and program to develop a mission statement. For congregations and programs, this needs to be accomplished collaboratively.

In their book *Youth Ministry Management Tools*, Mike Work and Ginny Olson talk about developing vision and mission statements for youth ministry programs. They emphasize first having a vision: "A vision is a picture of a preferred future, one that you're seeking to create. It should be only a couple of sentences and should be descriptive and challenging" (2014, 28). They then challenge leaders to articulate their vision: "The mission should be articulated in one or two clear, motivating statements that flow out of the vision and describe why you exist as a ministry" (2014, 29). One might argue that the mission should come first and then the vision, yet there is value in both. The mission articulates why you exist, and your vision describes what that mission looks like when lived out in real life. The mission statement should be succinct enough for people to remember and grasp it but broad enough to encompass all you do as a congregation or program. I find it helpful to have a list of goals that "flesh out" the mission.

A Personal Priority (Job Descriptions)

Jesus had clear priorities in His ministry (see above). He also helped the apostles to clarify their priorities as He trained them. In Acts 6, the apostles were confronted with the problem of Grecian widows not being taken care of in the Jerusalem "meals-on-wheels" program (supper-on-sandals?). They felt this was a problem that needed to be addressed; they made sure men were appointed to do so. It is interesting that they did not do it themselves because Jesus had given them a clear job description: "But we will devote ourselves to prayer and to the ministry of the word" (Acts 6:4). Jesus had given the apostles a responsibility to serve as witnesses of His life, death, and resurrection (cf. Acts 1:8). Had they devoted themselves to feeding the widows, they would have been doing a good work, but many people would have died without knowing how to go to heaven. Clarity in one's job description is important to success.

Leaders, it is important to have clear job descriptions for employees, workers, and volunteers. If you are an employee, worker, or volunteer, do everything in your power to get a job description for your areas of work. Many churches and religious organizations do not have clear job descriptions. I periodically serve as an evaluator on a visiting team for our academic accrediting agency (Association for Biblical Higher Education). My focus is on the board and administration of the school we are evaluating. One of my responsibilities is to make sure there are clear, written job descriptions for the senior administrators, especially the president. Not all universities have these. Only one of the five congregations I worked with in local work had a job description for my position, and it was literally handwritten. I typed it up to pass it on to the person who followed me at that congregation. Every elder, deacon, Bible class teacher, youth minister, preacher, etc. should get a job description.

I ask students I train to seek a job description from churches they are interviewing with. If the church does not have one, then I encourage the students to ask the elders and/or search committee to verbally go over what they expect from the person filling the position. I encourage the students to write down what the others are saying and to ask clarifying questions, if necessary. I then encourage the students to read the list back to the group to determine if what they heard is what the group intended. This is also an opportune time to discuss whether the demands of the position are reasonable. Once this process is completed, you then have a written job description that all have agreed upon.

Marlene Wilson, in her book *Volunteer Job Descriptions and Action Plans*, makes a couple of interesting observations. She states, "Until you can explain what a volunteer is supposed to do, most potential volunteers won't agree to come on board to give you a hand. Nor *should* they—because you aren't ready to put them to work doing something significant" (2004 *Job Descriptions*, 40). She then adds, "Recruiting volunteers before you design jobs is like trying to dance before the music starts. Sure, you can start dancing, but there's a good chance you'll end up out of step once the music begins" (2004 *Job Descriptions*, 41). (We will discuss job descriptions more in a later lesson.)

It is important to promote both mission statements and job descriptions. Former professor Flavil R. Yeakley, Jr. was right when he said, "In any institution the first responsibility of the chief administrative officer is to keep the focus of the organization on its central mission" (2014, 30). An archer cannot hit a target that is not set before him or her. If a congregation is going to live up to a mission, they need to know what the mission is. Once we established a mission statement at the Graymere church of Christ in Columbia, Tennessee, I would have a lesson near the beginning of each year focusing on our mission and goals. It is also important that members and workers have a general understanding of job responsibilities. This does not mean we share everything in a job description. It just means that there needs to be clarity among relevant participants on the area that each person is responsible for. When everyone knows their jobs and everyone else's jobs, there can be unity, and the work gets done.

Conclusion

Jesus said, "Can a blind man lead a blind man? Will they not both fall into a pit?" (Luke 6:39–40). Brother Bob Turner highlights six benefits of having a sense of vision in his book *Essential*:

1. Vision informs decision-making.
2. Vision promotes greater unity.
3. Vision kick-starts momentum.
4. Vision motivates the actions of life and leadership.
5. Vision creates meaning.
6. Vision challenges us to do something great (2020, 68–73).

The purpose of a compass is to help travelers to remember what direction is true north. If a person knows which direction is north, then he or she also knows where east, west, and south are. If we know what the right direction is, then it better enables us to recognize the wrong directions. Also, it helps us to differentiate between better and best. It is not always bad actions which keep us from doing what is most important. We are often so busy doing "good" things that we don't have time for the "best" things. What is our true north? What are we aiming at? If we do not know the answer to these questions, we may lead a whole church into a pit.

Discussion Questions

1. Does your congregation have a written mission statement? If not, why not?
2. If your congregation has a written statement, is it promoted to the congregation?
3. Does your congregation provide job descriptions to employees and volunteers? If not, why not?

Homework

1. I would like to challenge each person reading this book to take some time this week and make a list of the goals for your life. List your personal, family, and career goals. What are your leadership or ministry goals? Compare those goals with goals of Christ's life. Do they contradict one another? How do the activities of your everyday life fit with your goals? Does there need to be change?

2. Next, create a personal mission statement that encompasses your goals.

4

CONNECTED

HE HAD A PERSONAL RELATIONSHIP
WITH GOD

Introduction

IN HIS BOOK *Spiritual Disciplines for the Christian Life*, Donald S. Whitney states that the largest radio receiver in the world, known as VLA., is found in New Mexico. It is actually a cluster of twenty-seven massive telescopes working in unison to gather radio waves from millions of lightyears away. He notes that "the total energy of all radio waves ever recorded barely equals the force of a single snowflake hitting the ground" (Whitney 1991, 65). Human beings spend untold millions to probe the deepest recesses of space yet waste daily opportunities to communicate with the God who made all things.

It was my privilege to sit at the feet of Thomas H. Holland on several occasions while I was an undergraduate Bible student. In his book *Sermon Design and Delivery*, he reveals five criteria by which a minister can know his sermon is prepared. Number four on that list is the following:

Sermons are prepared when the preacher has prayed fervently about the sermon. (Acts 6:4). If the apostles thought that prayer was important in connection with the ministry of the Word, gospel preachers today should consider themselves extremely brazen if they refuse to plead for God's help (Holland 2000, 18–19).

I was also privileged to have a class under Billy Smith while I was a graduate student at Freed-Hardeman University. One of our textbooks for the class was *Between Two Worlds* by John R. W. Stott. Stott emphasized that preachers should pray over their messages before they deliver them. He states,

> It is on our knees before the Lord that we can make the message our own, possess or re-possess it until it possesses us. Then, when we preach it, it will come neither from our notes, nor from our memory, but out of the depths of our personal conviction, as an authentic utterance of our heart (Stott 1982, 257).

Jesus, the greatest preacher and leader, understood the value of prayer as well.

The Christ

Spiritual leadership must flow from a relationship with God. The simple truth is that a spiritual leader should not stand before God's people until he has knelt before their God. Jesus understood this well. It is interesting that we have no record of Jesus directly teaching His disciples how to teach or preach (the key word in that statement is "directly"). We do have a record of Him teaching them how to pray (Luke 11:1–4). We put so much emphasis on leadership styles and techniques that I fear we miss the key factor in spiritual leadership: A heart in intimate contact and communion with God. Jesus had such a heart. This lesson focuses on Jesus's contact with God through prayer.

It Was Personal

It is impossible for mere human beings to fathom the intimate relationship that exists between the Son and the Father. One senses this personal relationship in the prayer that Jesus prayed the night He was betrayed:

> I do not ask for these only, but also for those who will believe in me through their word, that they *may all be one, just as you, Father, are in me, and I in you,* that they also may be in us, so that the world may believe that you have sent me. The glory that you have given me I have given to them, *that they may be one even as we are one,* I in them and you in me, that they may become perfectly one, so that the world may know that you sent me and loved them *even as you loved me.* Father, I desire that they also, whom you have given me, may be with me where I am, to see my glory that you have given me because *you loved me before the foundation of the world.* O righteous Father, even though the world does not know you, *I know you,* and these know that you have sent me. I made known to them your name, and I will continue to make it known, *that the love with which you have loved me may be in them,* and I in them (John 17:20–26, emphasis mine).

Some describe Matthew 6:9–13 as "the Lord's prayer." That prayer is better titled as "the model prayer" or "the disciples' prayer." One of my former professors, Dr. Dowell Flatt, used to say that John 17 is the "real" Lord's prayer. This passage shows the Savior pouring out His heart to the Father as He prepares to fulfill His purpose on earth and face the cruelty of a Roman cross. This prayer is the second-longest prayer recorded in the Bible (second to Solomon's prayer at the dedication of the temple). This prayer reminds us of the intimate and personal relationship between the Father and the Son. Jesus's leadership flowed out of that intimate relationship.

Jesus, no doubt, longed for the full restoration of His relationship with the Father in heaven. You can almost hear the longing in Jesus's voice as He said, "I am coming to you" (John 17:11). When Jesus left this world, He went home. He told the religious leaders, "You are from below; I am from above. You are of this world; I am not of this world" (John 8:23). What do you do when you are away from family and friends? My guess is you that you make phone calls, or send texts, e-mails, or other types of electronic messages, so you can stay in touch. Jesus did the same thing through prayer.

It Was a Pattern

Imagine the incredible responsibility of saving the world. This is the burden that Jesus carried with Him on a daily basis. In addition to this responsibility and the normal pressures and frustrations of preaching and leadership, Jesus also struggled with a lack of privacy. People thronged to see Him everywhere He went. There were occasions in which He could not even eat because of the crowds of people (cf. Mark 6:31). His enemies constantly stalked Him, looking for an opportunity to trap Him (cf. Luke 5:12–39). His earthly ministry was filled with long days and sleepless nights. How would we deal with such pressure and fatigue?

Jesus dealt with it by talking to the Father on a regular basis. Consider the following example in Mark 1:32–38:

> That evening at sundown they brought to him all who were sick or oppressed by demons. And the whole city was gathered together at the door. And he healed many who were sick with various diseases, and cast out many demons. And he would not permit the demons to speak, because they knew him. And rising very early in the morning, while it was still dark, *he departed and went out to a desolate place, and there he prayed*. And Simon and those who were with him searched for him, and they found him and said to him, "Everyone is looking for you." And he said to them, "Let us go on to the next towns, that I may preach there also, for that is why I came out" (emphasis mine).

One reason Jesus was able to fulfill His mission on earth was that He kept in constant contact with the Father (cf. Mark 1:35 above). Another example of this is Luke 5:15–16: "But now even more the report about him went abroad, and *great crowds gathered to hear him* and to be healed of their infirmities. But *he would withdraw to desolate places and pray*" (emphasis mine). The Gospels make it clear that, through a pattern of prayer, Jesus was able to deal with the stress of saving the world.

He Prayed at the Pivotal Moments

Jesus's prayer life can be seen regularly in the pivotal and painful moments of His life. The Gospel of Luke has often been referred to as "the Gospel of prayer." It tells us more about the prayer life of Jesus than any other Gospel. Consider the following examples concerning the prayer life of Jesus:

- He prayed at His baptism (Luke 3:21).
- He prayed before choosing the Twelve (Luke 6:12–13, "all night he continued in prayer").
- He was praying before He asked, "Who do the crowds say that I am?" (Luke 9:18).
- He was praying during the transfiguration (Luke 9:28–29).
- He was praying when the disciples asked Him to teach them to pray (Luke 11:1).
- He prayed in the Garden (Luke 22:42).
- He prayed on the cross (Luke 23:34).

If one wishes to do further study on the prayer life of Jesus, he or she might read the ten recorded prayers of Jesus which are found in the New Testament:

1. Model prayer—Matt. 6:9–13; Luke 11:2–4 (differences show exactness in wording was not critical; attitude and ideas are the keys).
2. Praise prayer—Matt. 11:25–26; Luke 10:21.
3. Lazarus prayer—John 11:41–42.
4. Glorification prayer—John 12:28 (God responds).

5. Lord's prayer —John 17.
6. Peter's prayer—Luke 22:32 (doesn't give wording but subject matter).
7. Garden prayer —Luke 22:42, 44; Mark 14:36; Matt. 26:39, 42; Heb. 5:7.
   Cross prayers—Three of seven sayings at the cross were addressed to God.
8. Forgive prayer—Luke 23:34.
9. Forsaken prayer—Matt. 27:46; Mark 15:34.
10. Father prayer—Luke 23:46.

When we consider the prayers and prayer life of Jesus, it makes His statement on the cross all the more heartbreaking: "My God, my God, why have you forsaken me?" (Matt. 27:46). This statement is a quote from Psalm 22:1, which is a psalm of trust in God. This quote also reminds us that the great horror of the cross does not lie in the scourge, the nails, or the crown of thorns. It lies in the fact that the Christ, who treasured His relationship with the Father, was cut off from the Father for the first time in all of eternity. This happened because He was bearing the weight of my sins. One who gazes on the cross gets a small glimpse of what hell really is: separation from God ... silence from above!

The Christian

"Pay careful attention to yourselves and to all the flock, in which the Holy Spirit has made you overseers, to care for the church of God, which he obtained with his own blood" (Acts 20:28). Those words should send shivers up the spine of every elder in the Lord's church. Elders are in a position sanctioned by the Spirit of God to lead people bought by the blood of God! Spiritual leadership is serious business. This is not only true of elders; it is true of all positions of leadership in the church. Remember that Ephesians 4:11 teaches us that leadership positions in the church are gifts from Christ. This is a tremendous responsibility. The well-known 19th century Episcopalian minister and author of the song "O Little Town of Bethlehem," Phillips Brooks, rightly declared, "Do not pray for easy lives. Pray to be stronger men! Do not pray for tasks equal to your powers. Pray for powers equal to your tasks!" (1950, 352). It is only by the power of God that we can accomplish the task given to us.

Jesus not only modeled prayer, but He taught us to pray (Luke 11:1–4). He also called us to be people of prayer. In Luke 21:36 Jesus stated to the apostles, "But stay awake at all times, praying that you may have strength to escape all these things that are going to take place, and to stand before the Son of Man." Whitney highlights several passages that make it clear that Jesus expects us to pray (Matt. 6:5–9; Luke 11:9; 18:1). He then states,

> Suppose Jesus appeared to you personally, much as He did to the Apostle John on the Isle of Patmos in Revelation 1, and said that He expected you to pray. Wouldn't you become more faithful in prayer, knowing specifically that Jesus expected that of you? Well, the words of Jesus quoted above [in the passages listed] are as much His will for you as if He spoke your name and said them to you face to face (Whitney 1991, 67).

Jesus wanted His disciples to follow His example (cf. John

John 13:15). This also was true of the example He set in prayer.

I pray that this lesson will challenge us to examine our prayer lives. We need to begin by considering our congregational prayer habits. I think of the seven and a half years I spent working with the Graymere church of Christ in Columbia, Tennessee. The elders and preachers would meet once per month for a special time of prayer (of course we prayed at other times as well). We would discuss who had stopped worshiping and participating, who had been baptized or restored, who had married or had children, who had illnesses or surgeries, who was struggling with a problem, who had lost a loved one, and more. We would then divide up the names of each of these people among us and pray for them. It was special to hear godly men lifting up the names of their brothers and sisters to the throne of God. I think of special congregational prayer services we had which often featured our leaders praying about congregational needs. I also think of congregations I have worked with that prayed in the new year. We would establish a time of prayer on December 31 and let it flow into January 1. We would ask people to sign up for periods of prayer. We have done this at Heritage Christian University as well. It is powerful to know that people are praying about the congregation or school as the new year dawns. Our congregational prayer habits send messages about how we view the role of our heavenly Father and His power in what we do.

We need to also consider our personal prayer habits and ask ourselves some tough questions. How much time do we spend in prayer on the average day? Do we pray before we teach God's word or tackle some task for the Lord? Do we pray at the pivotal moments in our lives? Do we pray before important decisions? What is the longest we have prayed at any given time? Do we pray for ourselves and material things, or do we pray for the Lord to help us to be better servant-leaders for Him? The point is that a look at Jesus should always lead to a look at ourselves.

Jesus's ministry and teaching grew out of His relationship with God. Each of us has the opportunity to be the presence of God in the world. We cannot reveal a God that we do not know. To be His presence, we need to regularly go into His presence through prayer. We cannot speak of a God we do not speak to! Leaders must be people of prayer.

Conclusion

J. D. Walters is a friend of mine from Hatley, Mississippi. He once told me the story of walking by his brother Coy's room and overhearing him praying. J. D. said he stood at the door and thought to himself, "I wish I could pray like Coy." This same thing seems to have happened when the apostles saw Jesus praying in Luke 11:1–4. I hope that this lesson will inspire us to want to pray like Jesus. Jesus did not pray because He was commanded to do so. He prayed because He loved the One that He was talking to and longed for His companionship and strength. If the Messiah needed prayer, then should not we mere mortals avail ourselves of this tremendous honor of communing with the Creator of the universe?

Discussion Questions

1. Have you ever spent a day in prayer and fasting? If not, why not? Could this potentially help us to focus and get our hearts right as we consider important decisions?
2. Do the elders, deacons, and/or preachers in your congregation meet periodically to pray? If not, why not? If so, what kinds of things to you pray about?
3. How often does your congregation meet for special times of prayer (other than the normal prayers at the beginning and end of services)? What does this say to the members about how important prayer is to the leadership?

Homework

1. Read through the ten recorded prayers of Jesus that are listed in this chapter.
2. List three things you learned from the prayers of Jesus.

5

COMPASSIONATE

HE CARED FOR THOSE HE LED

Introduction

I REMEMBER well a doctoral class in which the professor asked us to talk about teachers who had impacted our lives. I talked about Dr. Rodney Cloud. I had taken a graduate class in Hebrew under Dr. Cloud a few years prior. I remember having a job conflict on the first day of class. It was my first class in Hebrew, and I was concerned about starting the semester three hours behind. Dr. Cloud invited me to his house. He prepared me a peanut butter and tomato sandwich (it is actually quite tasty!), personally tutored me on the information I would miss, and even made me a study cassette tape (younger readers will need to do a Google search for "cassette tape"). When I completed the class that semester, I decided I would take a Hebrew readings class the next semester. I did not yet know enough grammar to actually do much translating, so brother Cloud met with me on three occasions over the Christmas break to tutor me. I think of another teacher, Dr. Dennis Loyd, and his wife Shirley, who let me crash at their house for a week while taking another graduate course. I will always be indebted to these men and their families. Teaching for them was not about a paycheck; it was a passion. I will gladly listen to them teach on any subject for any amount of time because I know they genuinely care. The Gospel Advocate Company published a book on the life and work of the preacher titled *Man of God*. Jeffrey Dillinger authored the chapter which deals with the minister as "The Man of Compassion." He makes the following statement: "The man of God who is deficient in compassion deprives humanity of the heart of Christianity" (1996, 101). Compassion is at the heart of Christianity, it is at the heart of leadership, and it is at the heart of the ministry of Jesus.

The Christ

I was exposed to Kouzes and Posner while pursuing my doctorate. I found their landmark book, *The Leadership Challenge*, to be one of the finest books on leadership I had ever read. Their findings were based on solid research, but what stood out to me was how consistent their findings were with what I saw in Scripture. John C. Maxwell asked to use their research findings in one of his workshops, and that collaboration led to a follow-up book, *Christian Reflections on the Leadership Challenge* (which my friend, Mark Blackwelder, brought to my attention). In this sequel, they assert, "Leadership is a relationship," and go on to illustrate this in the ministry of Jesus.

> If Jesus had not been able to attract followers, Christianity might never have spread. And it was not just

the message that attracted followers; it was the man and his ability to engage with others. This may seem like an obvious point, but it's critical when we're talking about leadership, because the outcome of leadership is a result of the relationship (2004, 119).

With that in mind, let us focus in on Jesus's interaction with and compassion for people.

Personal

Henry and Richard Blackaby were correct when they stated, "Leadership is fundamentally about people! It is not merely about budgets or visions or strategies. It is about people" (Blackaby and Blackaby 2011, 39). Jesus took leadership personally. He knew that leadership was about relationships. God is the sovereign ruler of the universe, yet He seeks relationships with those He leads. God, the Son, "became flesh and dwelt among us" (John 1:14). In so doing, Jesus helped us to know God more intimately (cf. John 1:18; 14:6–7). One of the most beautiful statements of God's desire for intimacy is found in Jesus's prayer in John 17:

> Father, I desire that they also, whom you have given me, may be with me where I am, to see my glory that you have given me because you loved me before the foundation of the world. O righteous Father, even though the world does not know you, I know you, and these know that you have sent me. I made known to them your name, and I will continue to make it known,

that the love with which you have loved me may be in
them, and I in them (17:24–26).

Jesus's personal touch and desire for closeness can be
seen in several places in the Gospels.

The text of Matthew tells of five times that Jesus
personally "touched" someone: a leper, Peter's mother-in-
law who was sick with a fever, two blind men (twice), and
three apostles when terrified by the voice of God (Matt. 8:3,
15; 9:29; 17:7; 20:34). Jesus also took the daughter of Jairus
"by the hand" when He raised her (Matt. 9:25). Most of
these encounters involved healing someone. Jesus did not
even need to be present, much less touch someone, to heal
them (cf. Luke 7:1–10; 17:11–19). Jesus likely touched them
because He valued relationships. Touch would have been
especially important for a leper (Matt. 8:3). No one but
other lepers touched a leper. The miracle healed the leper
on the outside. The touch healed him on the inside. Jesus
ate in people's homes (Luke 10:38) and climbed into their
fishing boats (Luke 5:3). You may be familiar with the story
of Jesus using a little child as an illustration for one of His
sermons. Mark 9:36 tells us He took the child "in his arms."
Mark 10 records the powerful story of mothers bringing
their children to Jesus for a blessing and the disciples trying
to stop them. Not only did Jesus say, "Let the children come
to me," but He also "took them in his arms and blessed
them" (cf. Mark 10:14–16). Imagine a mother telling her
child years later, "You were once held by the Messiah!"
People mattered to Jesus, and He went out of His way
(including leaving heaven) to build relationships with them.
I cannot help but think of Jesus's words in John 10: "I am

the good shepherd. I know my own and my own know me" (10:14).

Purpose

An earlier chapter in this book considered Luke 4:18–19:

> The Spirit of the Lord is upon me, because he has anointed me to proclaim good news to the poor. He has sent me to proclaim liberty to the captives and recovering of sight to the blind, to set at liberty those who are oppressed, to proclaim the year of the Lord's favor.

This passage gives us the theme of the Gospel of Luke and the earthly sojourn of Christ. As we noted earlier, Christ came to preach and provide salvation. He also came to minister to the poor, captive, blind, and oppressed. God clothed Himself in the garment of human flesh and came to live among His creation (cf. John 1:14). Jesus told Philip, "Whoever has seen me has seen the Father" (John 14:9). Christ did not come just to tell people about the Father but to show them the Father and to show them that the Father loved them. Jesus prayed the night before His death,

> The glory that you have given me I have given to them, that they may be one even as we are one, I in them and you in me, that they may become perfectly one, *so that the world may know that you sent me and loved them even as you loved Me* (John 17:22–23; emphasis mine).

As Jesus touched the poor, captive, blind, and oppressed, humanity was able to see that God cared. Jesus showed that God's love includes those individuals who are cast aside by the world. Truly God "loved the world" (John 3:16). Having gazed upon Christ, human beings are now able to echo the words of Job, "I had heard of you by the hearing of the ear, but now my eye sees You" (Job 42:5).

The chief trait of Jesus's character was love (cf. Eph. 5:2). He looked upon a rich young ruler and "loved him" (Mark 10:21). He loved Mary, Martha, and Lazarus (John 11:35–36). He loved His apostles (John 13:1). His love for all He encountered is seen in the ten references in the Gospels to Jesus having compassion. Jesus also tells two parables which highlight the compassion of God: the unmerciful servant (Matt. 18:23–27) and the prodigal son (Luke 15:11–20). To have compassion (Greek *splanchnídzomai*) means "have pity, feel sympathy" (Danker 2000, 938). Thayer's lexicon highlights the root of the word when it says it means "properly, to be moved as to one's bowels, hence to be moved with compassion, have compassion, (for the bowels were thought to be the seat of love and pity)" (Thayer 1889, 584). Thus, we see that Christ was touched deep inside by the hurts and needs of others. Our next section will focus on some specific examples of Christ's compassion. Before we move on, let us emphasize that showing love and compassion were part of Christ's purpose on earth.

Practice

Dillinger reminds us that compassion is more than just a deep-seated feeling for the hurts of others: "Compassion is action toward men, whereas pity and sympathy are feelings. Compassion extends beyond emotion and tries to eliminate or alleviate the dilemma" (1996, 101). Lawrence O. Richards and Gary J. Bredfeldt add, "There are many ways love can be expressed. But *real* love must be expressed" (1998, 232). The point is that compassion and love are action words. I am reminded of the words of John in 1 John 3:18: "Little children, let us not love in word or talk but in deed and in truth." Christ put His love into action. That is what compassion is. Let us consider some examples of Christ's love in action:

- Matt. 9:35–36 (Teaching around Galilee; cf. Mark 6:34).
- Matt. 14:14–15 (Feeding of 5,000).
- Matt. 15:32 (Feeding of 4,000; cf. Mark 8:2).
- Matt. 20:33–34 (Blind men at Jericho).
- Mark 1:41–42 (A leper).
- Mark 5:19–20 (The Gadarene demoniac).
- Luke 7:13–15 (Raising the widow of Nain's son).

The depth of Christ's compassion can be seen in His triumphant entry into Jerusalem. Fisher shares some beautiful thoughts as he describes Jesus's riding down the side of a hill looking across at the city that would kill Him:

> Luke tells us that as Jesus rode down the hill into the city he looked at it and began to weep and sob. "If you, even you, had only known on this day what would bring you peace ..." (Luke 19:42). He could have ridden down that hill, filled with resentment and anger for a culture that suppressed the Word of God, opposed and killed God's

prophets, and would murder him within a week. Instead he entered the city with a broken heart. Christ's church and its pastoral leaders need to follow Jesus down that hill toward our address (1996, 41).

The poet Lord Byron wrote the following in a poem called *The Tear*: "Mild Charity's glow, / To us mortals below, / Shows the soul from barbarity clear; / Compassion will melt, / Where this virtue is felt, / And its dew is diffused in a Tear" (1882, 11). Byron was saying that the dew of compassion is a tear. Christ's visit to Jerusalem shows not only a Savior who poured forth the dew of compassion but also a Savior who wept those tears for the very people who would take His life. I can do nothing more than stand in awe of such love.

The biblical record tells of throngs of people coming to meet and listen to Jesus (twenty-seven times in Matthew alone; cf. Matt. 4:25; 5:1; 8:1; 9:8, 33, 36, etc.). Why did these people go to such great lengths to hear a poor carpenter who had no rabbinical training and was from a city with a poor reputation? There are many answers that might be given, but I think one reason was that He was compassionate. Note the following:

> And he went throughout all Galilee, teaching in their synagogues and proclaiming the gospel of the kingdom and healing every disease and every affliction among the people. *So his fame spread throughout all Syria*, and they brought him all the sick, those afflicted with various diseases and pains, those oppressed by demons, those having seizures, and paralytics, and he healed them. *And great crowds followed him* from Galilee and the Decapolis,

and from Jerusalem and Judea, and from beyond the Jordan (Matt. 4:23–25, emphasis mine).

Many people heard the good news because Jesus healed. They came because He cared.

The Christian

Now it is time to apply this chapter to ourselves as Christian leaders. Automobile tycoon Henry Ford once said, "You can take my factories, burn up my buildings, but give me my people, and I'll bring my business right back again" (qtd. in Maxwell 1995, 12). If your house were on fire and you could choose to get your family out or your computer and iPhone out, which would you choose? If you had to choose between saving the building in which your congregation meets and the people who worship in the building, which would you choose? I assume you would choose your family and the people. If so, why is it we invest so much time in buildings and technology and so little time in people?

Let's Get Personal

We must make leadership personal. Godly leaders value relationships. Maxwell observed, "People are interested in the person who is interested in them" (2004, 88). Are we genuinely interested in people, or do we use people as a means to an end? This is a challenge for those who do fundraising. I prefer the term "friendraising" over fundraising. I had a text conversation with our Administrative Council while writing this book. I had learned of a family that had made a major donation to Heritage Christian University fifteen years before I came to work with the school. The gift was the second most any family had ever given to us. I asked about family members to whom I could say thank you. During the conversation, Pat Moon, our Senior Vice President of Administration, talked about how important relationships are with donors. Here was my response:

> You are so right about the importance of relationships. I think we just love people and let God provide the increase. We have to treasure the relationship even if they never give us a dime (or need to stop giving). If they know that we genuinely care, then what matters to us will matter to them.

That statement is my philosophy of fundraising in a nutshell. It is also my philosophy of leadership.

Leaders must invest in relationships. It is not about sitting in a room and making decisions that impact other people's lives. We need to get out of our boardrooms and into people's living rooms. We need to get out of our offices and into hospital rooms, nursing homes, and funeral homes. I have frequently told the preachers I have trained that we earn the right to be heard on Sunday by loving into people's lives on Monday through Saturday. People will put up with many a poorly delivered sermon (although not one with false doctrine) if they know we truly care about them. The first summer I worked at Heritage Christian University, I met personally with all of our employees to try and get to know them. There are natural apprehensions any time you have a change in leadership, especially when people do not know the new leader. I made sure these meetings were not in my office so people would not be afraid they were about to lose their jobs. We called the meetings "Cookies, Coffee, and Conversation" in an attempt to alleviate concerns. It is still a work in process, but I do want to know our people better, and I pray that in time we can all become friends.

Visiting hurting people was always important to me when I served as a preacher or youth minister in a congregation. Now that I no longer serve in those roles, I am grateful when time and opportunity allow me to visit with members of congregations I worked with in the past. When I show up at the hospital or funeral home, they can see that I truly care about them. They understand that I do not visit members because it is a job. I visit because they are my friends and my brothers and sisters in Christ.

We need to invest in really getting to know the people we work with. Sheer numbers may prevent us from knowing everyone with equal intimacy, but we should know those we work with most closely well and do our best to develop relationships with as many others as possible. Maxwell lists six things that can help us to show people that they matter to us:

1. Become genuinely interested in other people.
2. Smile.
3. Remember that a person's name is to him or her the sweetest and most important sound.
4. Be a good listener—encourage others to talk about themselves.
5. Talk in terms of the other person's interests.
6. Make the other person feel important, and do it sincerely. (2004, 90–94)

My girls bought me an edited version of the HBO mini-series *Band of Brothers* a few years ago (edited out language and nudity). The series included interviews with actual members of Easy Company of the 101st Airborne. I remember a statement made by First Lieutenant Lynn "Buck" Compton in his interview: "A good leader has to understand the people that are under them, understand their needs, their desires, or how they think a little bit." Spiritual leaders need to know the people around them. Time together and listening are two of the best ways to do that.

Getting Personal in a Pandemic

The COVID-19 pandemic has made it more difficult to build and maintain relationships. There are several things we are learning in this pandemic. We are learning who is committed to Christ and who is not. We are learning who cares about others and who cares about themselves. Just as fire tests the purity of precious metals, so adversity tests true faith and true love. We are learning the value of relationships. Our students at HCU were very excited to be back on campus in the fall of 2020. It was tough on all of us when they had to go home in mid-March of that year because of COVID-19. We put a number of restrictions in place for their return. During our first chapel of the year, I asked our student body president at the time, Kaleb Baker, how the students were doing with regulations. He said something along the lines of the following: "If you wanted us to wear full hazmat suits, we would wear them. We are just glad to be here." Relationships matter.

Several churches found a disconnect with a large

portion of their membership during the crisis. There might be several reasons for this. The disconnected could be members who were not truly committed in the first place (cf. 1 Cor. 11:19). It also could be that they did not feel they had lost anything. Maybe they felt there was no investment in them or that they were not important to the congregation or leadership before the pandemic, so when churches began having virtual gatherings instead of physical gatherings, they did not feel they had lost anything. Many people attend worship week after week and feel alone and ignored even though they are in a crowd of people.

Another problem might be that leadership did not invest in continuing the relationship by new means during the pandemic. Leaders must be willing to adapt. Just because we cannot connect in the ways that are normal to us does not mean we have an excuse not to connect. I have heard stories of people sitting in chairs outside people's windows at nursing homes, signs being posted in someone's yard, friends and church leaders gathering outside a window to pray, and drive-by parades to show love. Where possible, some delivered food to people. Others sent cards, made calls, sent texts, sent emails, and had Zoom and Facetime conversations. Several of our leaders at the congregation my family worships with stayed in touch with us through several means during our time apart. Technology provides many opportunities to connect. This technology was used by many to produce online lessons. The common joke has been that every preacher is now a televangelist. There are multiple apps and digital access platforms that allow individuals to stay in communication with one another when face-to-face interaction is not possible. We just need to take the time to learn and use them. All you have to do is go to YouTube or do a simple Google search, and you can find all kinds of ways to communicate with people and training on how to do so. Aubrey Johnson did his doctoral work in the area of leadership and has produced some excellent writing on leadership in the church. In one of his books, *Successful Shepherds*, Johnson makes a very helpful comment relative to learning to use technology:

> If you are not technologically proficient, the good news is that someone is eager and willing to assist if you ask for help. What a wonderful way to connect with younger people in the church. Let them mentor you in technology while you mentor them spiritually. Talk about win-win. This is intergenerational church at its best (Johnson 2019, Kindle location 1528).

Ignorance is not an excuse. Godly leaders value people and will invest any amount of time necessary in connecting to them and learning alternative ways to connect when something happens to interfere with the normal means of communication.

Let's Practice Compassion

Consider the words of Peter:

> Finally, all of you, have unity of mind, sympathy, brotherly love, a tender heart, and a humble mind. Do not repay evil for evil or reviling for reviling, but on the contrary, bless, for to this you were called, that you may obtain a blessing (1 Peter 3:8–9).

The heart of what it means to be a leader can be found in the famous words of Theodore Roosevelt: "People don't care how much you know until they know how much you care" (quoted in Meeks 2017, 147). Do the people we lead know that we care? Do the people in our congregations know that we care?

People follow people they trust. People tend to trust leaders whom they believe genuinely care about them. Simon Sinek, in his book *Leaders Eat Last*, talks about this concept:

> Leaders are the ones willing to look out for those to the left of them and those to the right of them. They are often willing to sacrifice their own comfort for ours, even when they disagree with us. Trust is not simply a matter of shared opinions. Trust is a biological reaction to the belief that someone has our well-being at heart. Leaders are the ones who are willing to give up something of their own for us. Their time, their energy, their money, maybe even the food off their plate. When it matters, leaders choose to eat last. (2017, 82–83)

I often note who goes first at church potlucks. I try hard to make sure that I eat near the end of the line (though sometimes I eat earlier when I am the speaker after the meal). It is in the mundane things of life, like a congregational potluck, that we show if we are selfish or a servant. Compassion is about putting others before ourselves. It is about noticing their needs and doing something to ease their pain. Maxwell was correct when he stated, "One of the greatest remedies for our own suffering is serving others.

Servant-leadership becomes a solution for both the one serving and the one being served" (2007, 1198).

Sinek stresses that leaders "only become leaders when they accept the responsibility to protect those in their care" (2017, 83). Elders, for example, are asked to shepherd God's people, God's flock (cf. Acts 20:28). This includes protecting them from spiritual wolves (Acts 20:29–30). Leaders also help to protect those who follow them from physical and emotional wolves and sometimes from each other. The members of our congregations need to know that we will be there for them when they are hungry, hurting, and heartbroken. The people in our communities need to know that we care about their pain. *Compassion might be described as hurt for the hurt of others, which flows out of love and flows into action.* In other words, compassion is an action word. We do not just feel it; we show it, we do it. We show it to our fellow Christians when we visit the nursing home and funeral home, when we show up in the emergency room after a car accident, when we set up late at night to encourage a couple whose marriage is on the rocks, and when we step in to help members financially as they go through the loss of their jobs. We show it to our communities when we stop to fix a tire for someone we have never met, when we volunteer with our local *Room at the Inn* program for the homeless, when we take food to the hungry, or when we help to promote justice and equality for those in our communities who live every day with bigotry, unkindness, and racism. How many avoid church buildings all across this country because they do not think the people inside care about them? But if we will invest in them, love them, then amazing things can happen. In his book *Relationships 101*, Maxwell states,

Once you understand people and believe in them, they can really become somebody. And it doesn't take much effort to make people feel important. Little things, done deliberately at the right time, can make a big difference (2003, 17).

Conclusion

There is a framed piece of notebook paper in my office that says, "I want to be a garbage man." When I was in high school, we would vote on what we called "senior superlatives." These "awards" for the senior class focused on things like most athletic, friendliest, most likely to succeed, etc. We would also have a senior spaghetti supper at the end of the year in which we celebrated our years together. This usually included making fun of those who won awards (to make sure our heads did not grow too large). At this point, I should also mention another custom we had in high school. We would secretly stick signs on each other's backs. These might say things like "I need a date for the prom" or "Kick me." On the night of our supper, they made me wear the sign that I now have framed in my office: "I want to be a garbage man." To my friends, that was the opposite of success. I kept that sign for two reasons: (1) so I would never look down on a person who earns an honest day's living, and (2) because I believe Jesus was a garbage man.

Garbage collectors take what other people do not want. That is what Jesus did. He collected the people that society had thrown away. Think of the countless lepers, blind, lame, deaf, mute, demon-possessed, Samaritans, women, and children who encountered Christ. They were unvalued or undervalued in the society in which they lived, but they were treasured by Jesus. He did not collect them to simply transport them to some kind of spiritual landfill, out of sight and out of mind. He collected them and introduced them to His Father. People came to hear Jesus speak, in part, because they knew He loved them. I began this lesson telling about teachers who had impacted my life. If someone had asked the question, "What teacher has had an impact on your life?" at Capernaum, Nazareth, or Jerusalem two thousand years ago, there might well have been a leper, a demon-possessed woman, or a little boy who liked to eat bread and fish who would have told a story about a carpenter from Galilee. Is there anyone who will answer that question with your name or my name? If we want the world to come to Christ, we must have hearts filled with the compassion of Christ.

Discussion Questions

1. Why do you think we tend to reduce leadership to decisions made in a boardroom?
2. What could your congregation do to better serve minorities or the homeless?
3. How does your congregation divide up the areas of work for deacons? How much is this driven by the needs of the community or congregation?

Homework

1. Read through the compassion passages listed in this chapter and make a list of things that stood out to you in those passages.

2. Read John 10:1–18 and make a list of things that stood out to you about the leadership of Jesus.

3. Make a list of the top ten needs in your community and in your congregation. Propose a possible response for at least three of those needs.

6

COMMON
HE HAD A HUMBLE HEART

Introduction

Two DUCKS and a frog lived together on a pond and became good friends. When the summer heat began to dry up the pond, the ducks decided that they needed to move on. This was not so easy for the frog. He could not fly. The frog suggested the ducks might fly with a stick that they each held in their bills. The frog could hold on to the middle of the stick with his mouth. The plan was working perfectly until a farmer looked up and saw the ducks and frog flying over. "Well, isn't that a clever idea!" he said. "I wonder who thought of it?" The frog replied: "I diiiiid. ..." Splat! ("Two Ducks" 1989, 34). True is the proverb, "Pride goes before destruction, and a haughty spirit before a fall" (Prov. 16:18).

Paul adds, "Therefore let anyone who thinks he stands take heed lest he fall" (1 Cor. 10:12). Those words need to be in the heart of all those who dare to lead the people of God! Stott rightly stated,

We stand there in solitude, while the eyes of all are upon us. We hold forth in monologue, while all sit still, silent and subdued. Who can endure such public exposure and remain unscathed by vanity? Pride is without doubt the chief occupational hazard of the preacher. It has ruined many, and deprived their ministry of power (1982, 320).

John MacArthur highlights the leadership of the apostle Paul in his book *Called to Lead*. Having discussed Paul's comments in 1 Corinthians 15:10 and 2 Corinthians 3:5, MacArthur sets forth the following principle: "A leader knows his own limitations." He explains, "Those whom the world holds up as leaders often exude arrogance, cockiness, egotism, and conceit. Those things are not qualities of true leadership; they are actually hindrances to it" (2004, 101).

One of the greatest dangers for leaders is to be conquered by pride. We have hinted at the humility of Jesus in earlier chapters, but I felt we would be remiss if we did not devote at least one full chapter to this important character trait of the Son of God. Let us first turn our attention to Christ, and then we will shift to the Christian.

The Christ

In his landmark book on leadership, *Good to Great*, Jim Collins highlights the traits that are present in great companies that are different from the traits in just good companies. (He has very specific criteria for which companies are in each category.) He identifies five levels of leadership that exist in companies: Level 1 – "Highly Capable Individual," Level 2 – "Contributing Team Member," Level 3 – "Competent Manager," Level 4 – "Effective Leader," and Level 5

– "Level 5 Executive" (Collins 2001, 20). He observes that the great companies tend to have Level 5 Executives. The Level 5 Executive builds "enduring greatness through a paradoxical blend of personal humility and professional will" (Collins 2001, 20). Collins goes on to add, "Level 5 leaders channel their ego needs away from themselves and into the larger goal of building a great company" (2001, 21). With success, there is a danger of thinking too highly of ourselves. Great churches, like great companies, are built by leaders who are willing to put their egos aside. In our study thus far, we have stressed the incredible abilities and character traits of Jesus as a leader. We have noted how people often followed Him in droves. Had we been in the same circumstances, we might have been overcome with pride. Jesus preached and practiced otherwise.

Preaching

Humility was at the heart of Jesus's teaching. Most of us have heard the expression, "First come, first served." Jesus turned this saying upside down. He taught, "First come, last served" or "Serve first, then come." If we rush to the front, we will be moved to the back. Consider the following:

> For from within, out of the heart of man, come evil thoughts, sexual immorality, theft, murder, adultery, coveting, wickedness, deceit, sensuality, envy, slander, *pride*, foolishness. All these evil things come from within, and they defile a person (Mark 7:21–23, emphasis mine).

> And they came to Capernaum. And when he was in the house he asked them, "What were you discussing on the

way?" But they kept silent, *for on the way they had argued with one another about who was the greatest.* And he sat down and called the twelve. And he said to them, "*If anyone would be first, he must be last of all and servant of all.*" And he took a child and put him in the midst of them, and taking him in his arms, he said to them, "Whoever receives one such child in my name receives me, and whoever receives me, receives not me but him who sent me" (Mark 9:33–37, emphasis mine).

And James and John, the sons of Zebedee, came up to him and said to him, "Teacher, we want you to do for us whatever we ask of you." And he said to them, "What do you want me to do for you?" And they said to him, "Grant us to sit, one at your right hand and one at your left, in your glory." Jesus said to them, "You do not know what you are asking. Are you able to drink the cup that I drink, or to be baptized with the baptism with which I am baptized?" And they said to him, "We are able." And Jesus said to them, "The cup that I drink you will drink, and with the baptism with which I am baptized, you will be baptized, but to sit at my right hand or at my left is not mine to grant, but it is for those for whom it has been prepared." And when the ten heard it, they began to be indignant at James and John. And Jesus called them to him and said to them, "You know that those who are considered rulers of the Gentiles lord it over them, and their great ones exercise authority over them. But it shall not be so among you. *But whoever would be great among you must be your servant, and whoever would be first among you must be slave of all. For even the Son of Man came not to be served but to serve, and to give his life as a ransom for many*" (Mark 10:35–45, emphasis mine).

The apostles and disciples of Jesus struggled with pride. That was what they saw in the leaders of the world in which they lived. This was true whether they looked to the Pharisees and Sadducees or the leaders of the Roman empire. The pagan leaders lorded over those who followed (Mark 10:42). Notice Jesus's words to the disciples: "But it shall not be so among you" (Mark 10:43). Jesus was breaking the leadership mold. He broke the mold in so many other areas of life, why should it be any different with leadership? As with the other changes He called for, the disciples struggled to pour themselves into this new mold. It was going to take more than preaching to change them.

Practice

If anyone ever had the right to be proud, it was Jesus. However, His practices show that He was anything but arrogant. In the Philippian letter, Paul challenged the brethren to be people of humility.

> So if there is any encouragement in Christ, any comfort from love, any participation in the Spirit, any affection and sympathy, complete my joy by being of the same mind, having the same love, being in full accord and of one mind. *Do nothing from selfish ambition or conceit, but in humility count others more significant than yourselves.* Let each of you look not only to his own interests, but also to the interests of others (Phil. 2:1–4, emphasis mine).

For Paul, the keys to unity were how we view ourselves and how we view others. He saw humility as a glue that holds God's people together. He then gave Jesus as an example to motivate them to carry out this command.

> *Have this mind among yourselves, which is yours in Christ Jesus,* who, though he was in the form of God, did not count equality with God a thing to be grasped, but *emptied himself*, by taking the form of a servant, being born in the likeness of men. And being found in human form, *he humbled himself* by becoming obedient to the point of death, even death on a cross. Therefore God has highly exalted him and bestowed on him the name that is above every name, so that at the name of Jesus every knee should bow, in heaven and on earth and under the earth, and every tongue confess that Jesus Christ is Lord, to the glory of God the Father (Phil. 2:5–11, emphasis mine).

We will never fully understand what Jesus gave up. Paul described it this way in the letter we commonly call 2 Corinthians: "For you know the grace of our Lord Jesus Christ, that though he was rich, yet for your sake he became poor, so that you by his poverty might become rich" (8:9). He left the glories of heaven to be born in a place where animals were kept (probably a cave), laid in a feeding trough, raised in poverty, and crucified on a tree that He made as Creator of the world (John 1:3). He "became poor" so we "might become rich" (2 Cor. 8:9). This sacrifice is what Paul was trying to describe to the Philippian Christians when he said Jesus "emptied himself." Jesus is the ultimate example of humility.

When one thinks of the humility of Jesus, there is one

key passage that should immediately come to mind. Outside of Dallas Theological Seminary in Dallas, Texas, is a bronze statue of Jesus washing the feet of one of the disciples. It is a beautiful work of art and theology. I took a picture so I would not forget it, but the reality is that I will not forget it whether I ever look at that picture again or not. It is that image that comes into my mind when I hear the word "humble." It is a picture of the Savior of the world wrapped in a towel and washing feet. I am a visual learner; thus, movies often help me to understand and process things. I remember this scene in the *Gospel of John* movie. Watching Jesus bathe their feet and, in particular, seeing the looks on the apostles' faces as He did so was a moving and humbling experience. Try to create a mental picture in your mind as we read John's account of this amazing event.

> Now before the Feast of the Passover, when Jesus knew that his hour had come to depart out of this world to the Father, having loved his own who were in the world, he loved them to the end. During supper, when the devil had already put it into the heart of Judas Iscariot, Simon's son, to betray him, Jesus, knowing that the Father had given all things into his hands, and that he had come from God and was going back to God, rose from supper. He laid aside his outer garments, and taking a towel, tied it around his waist. Then he poured water into a basin and began to wash the disciples' feet and to wipe them with the towel that was wrapped around him (John 13:1–5).

In *The Maxwell Leadership Bible,* Maxwell makes the following comments about the opening verses of John 13:

Jesus knew who He was, and He was secure enough to get down on the floor and wash His disciples' feet. He didn't have to prove anything. In fact, He had nothing to prove, nothing to lose, and nothing to hide. The insecure are into titles. The secure are into towels (2007, 1326).

What makes this account even more amazing are the circumstances under which Jesus performs this act of service and the consideration of whose feet He washed. Jesus was just hours from the cross. Even then, He was thinking of others. Think of the feet He washed. He washed the feet of men that He created (cf. John 1:1–4). He also washed the feet of men who would forsake Him and flee when He was taken prisoner. One of them, one who was among His closest friends, would deny knowing Him. Another would betray Him to His enemies. It was this humble servant attitude which separated Jesus from the religious teachers of His day.

Maxwell notes, "Often we assume that if we serve, people will lower their view of us; that they will assume we possess the lowest position in the organization. But this is wrong." After giving mothers as examples, he adds,

People are drawn toward those who serve them sacrificially, not repelled by them. Service adds value to people. Servanthood is not about position or skill. It's about attitude. Leaders seek ways they can add value to others, and the primary way they do it is by serving them (2007, 1326).

To prove Maxwell's point, consider Jesus Himself. Jesus

lived a life of humble service to others, and millions of people have followed Him!

The Christian

Why did Jesus wash the disciples' feet? Let us return to the story in John 13 before we answer that question:

> When he had washed their feet and put on his outer garments and resumed his place, he said to them, "Do you understand what I have done to you? You call me Teacher and Lord, and you are right, for so I am. If I then, your Lord and Teacher, have washed your feet, you also ought to wash one another's feet. *For I have given you an example, that you also should do just as I have done to you*" (John 13:12–15, emphasis mine).

Remember that Jesus had to repeatedly deal with the arrogance of the disciples. They literally argued over which one of them was greatest (Mark 9:34). Jesus had taught them to be humble, yet they still struggled. How would He break this cycle of pride? With a towel and a basin of water. Notice again His words, "For I have given you an example, that you also should do just as I have done to you" (John 13:15). In so doing, He also set an example for us. We too, if we are to lead like the Lord, must be people of humility.

I have had the privilege of teaching at three of our accredited brotherhood liberal arts schools and two preaching schools. I have worked with some amazing young people. It is exciting to think about how God is going to use them to do amazing things. I love them and thank God for the privilege of knowing them. There is also a disease I see in some of the Bible majors graduating from our schools. It is called "iamititus." Let me slow it down, so you can hear the pronunciation: "I-am-it-itus." Sometimes we think that because we have a diploma saying we have a degree in Bible that we are God's gift to the world. Because we have studied in a classroom at a university or preaching school, we assume that we know more than those who "only" studied in their bedrooms or around a kitchen table. How can a farmer or a schoolteacher possibly know the Bible as well as us? They have not studied hermeneutics, homiletics, or biblical languages, have they? Who cares that they may have studied the Bible for 40 years and may have experienced things in life that we will not come to understand for decades? Some of those who graduate from preacher training schools think that they are better than those who graduate from liberal arts Bible programs and vice versa. Each has its own reason for looking down on the other. It is one thing to be proud of and to believe in your school. Arrogance is a whole other ball game. Pride is not only a trait of younger preachers. Many older preachers have failed to teach and exemplify humility to those coming along behind them. God forbid that arrogance should find its way into our pulpits!

I issue a challenge to all brotherhood schools, of any type, who are training preachers to fill our pulpits. Train foot washers, not Pharisees. Likewise, as more and more congregations and summer camps are training young people to teach classes and lead in worship, there is a tremendous coinciding danger of arrogance. I believe we should encourage and give honor to whom honor is due, but if our young people see ministry as something we do for trophies and accolades, then we have totally missed what the biblical concept of leadership and ministry is all about. There is a very fine line between confidence and arrogance. I am a strong believer in preacher and leadership training programs for young people, but we must make sure that teaching humility is a key component of those programs. It must be more than just a passing comment made in one class. It must be constantly stressed and modeled before those being trained until it becomes part of their spiritual DNA.

Thus far, those who are not preachers or teachers may have thought they were going to get off easy in this lesson. I am sorry, but that is not the case. Arrogance is deadly disease that every Christian must fight, not just preachers. Those in positions of leadership, in particular, will be especially susceptible to this evil virus. On occasion, elders and deacons will let their positions go to their heads. Elders sometimes forget that their authority lies in the group, not in each one as an individual. Deacons may forget that the very title they wear means "servant." Brad Lomenick, in his work *H3 Leadership*, makes an insightful observation:

> Many leaders will tell you they don't believe the universe —or even their department—revolves around them. But if you pop the organization's hood, you'll see a different picture. The team may not feel free to challenge the leader's opinion. The company's procedures may require the leader's approval or signature before even minor decisions can be finalized. Or the culture requires constant praise and approval of the leader (2015, 25).

As church leaders, we need to think about whether we

are creating congregational cultures which are leader-centered or Lord-centered.

Think of other ways in which we have prideful attitudes toward others and may not consciously realize it. We look down on those from other religious groups. We look down on those who respond to the invitation often. We look down on those who are guilty of what we label as "big sins." We look down on people with different incomes, or in different educational or social levels from us. We look down on those who seek benevolence help. We look down on people from different countries, races, cultures, and genders. We even look down on people based on where they live, where they went to high school, or what sports team they follow. If we are not careful, arrogant attitudes will creep into our hearts and ooze out in our conduct and conversations.

Paul told Titus,

> For we ourselves were once foolish, disobedient, led astray, slaves to various passions and pleasures, passing our days in malice and envy, hated by others and hating one another. But when the goodness and loving kindness of God our Savior appeared, He saved us (Titus 3:3–5).

To stay humble, we need to remember our mistakes and our weaknesses and what God has done for us in spite of those mistakes. We need to remember that all human beings are made in the image of God. Most of all, we need to keep our focus on Jesus and follow His example.

Conclusion

F. B. Meyer observed,

> I used to think God's gifts were on shelves—one above the other and the taller we grew, the more easily we could reach them. I now find that God's gifts are on shelves one beneath the other and that it is not a question of growing taller but of stooping lower (quoted in McLellan 2000, 134).

Over and over, the Bible calls us to be people of humility. James summed up God's message well when he said, "God opposes the proud but gives grace to the humble" (James 4:6). Where did James learn this reality? Maybe he learned it from the example and teaching of his brother, Jesus (cf. Matt. 23:12). We have all heard the old saying that says we should not judge another until we have walked a mile in their shoes. Jesus teaches us to do more than just walk in another's shoes. He teaches me to take those shoes off and wash their feet.

Discussion and Homework

In his book *H3 Leadership*, Lomenick challenges leaders to consider the following questions to identify whether they have created an organization that revolves around them:

- Are others required to consult you before making basic decisions?
- Do you find yourself using the word *I* excessively?

- Must others keep you in the loop about details that do not directly affect your job?
- Do you have many trusted advisors who have permission to critique your decisions?
- Do you require regular applause and affirmation?
- Are people afraid to risk due to fear of backlash from you?
- Do you resist sharing blame if something goes awry?
- Do your receive criticism as regularly as you offer it to others? (25)

Recognizing that these questions are aimed primarily at contexts outside of the church, consider the following:

1. Reflect on how you would answer these questions personally. Think of possible changes you may need to make based on how you would answer these questions.
2. Are these questions relevant in a congregational setting? Why or why not?
3. Discuss how we find balance between exercising oversight over those who follow us and creating a self-centered world where all decisions run through us and we do not trust others to make decisions.

7

CLEAR THINKING
HE MADE WISE DECISIONS

Introduction

Up until I started studying for my doctorate, my training had been in Scripture, theology, preaching, communication, and ministry in the local church. With my final degree, I was exposed to the educational world and research that would have been handy to know about in my first 20 years of work in local congregations as a preacher and youth minister. I was exposed to Jean Piaget's work on the biological development of the brain and Lev Vygotsky's research on the social development of the human mind. Along the way, I learned about the insights from Howard Gardner in the area of human intelligence. Piaget identified biological stages that the mind goes through. Vygotsky highlighted the impact of environment on a person's thinking. Gardner challenged us to go beyond focusing on logical intelligence to thinking in terms of multiple intelligences (musical, linguistic, mechanical, etc.).

Paul, the apostle, knew something about the development of the mind. He stated, "When I was a child, I spoke like a child, I thought like a child, I reasoned like a child. When I became a man, I gave up childish ways" (1 Cor. 13:11). Just as Paul's mind had developed as he grew physically, Paul knew that our minds need to develop as we grow spiritually. In Philippians 2:5 he said, "Have this mind among yourselves, which is yours in Christ Jesus." Frederick W. Danker's lexicon tells us that "mind" (*phronéo*) means "to have an opinion with regard to something, think, form/hold an opinion, judge" (2000, 1065). Paul was calling Christians to think like Jesus.

As leaders for God, we must learn to think like Jesus. We need to develop wise, clear thinking, spiritual minds that can make decisions that are best for the people and mission of God. After discussing Gardner's multiple intelligences theory, Mohler talks about the need for leaders to have what he calls "convictional intelligence." He states, "Convictional intelligence is the product of learning the Christian faith, diving deeply into biblical truth, and discovering how to think like a Christian" (2012, 31). He notes that we "operate out of intellectual reflexes" (2012, 34). In light of this, he says,

> The Christian leader must have mental reflexes that correspond to biblical truth. When something happens or an issue arises, the leader's mind must activate the right intellectual reflex. Once that reflex is engaged, the process of thought is already far down the road. If the reflex is wrong, the leader is in danger—and so are all those he leads (2012, 34).

Let us take a moment and consider the mental reflexes of the Son of God.

The Christ

Who is the wisest man to ever live? Did Solomon's name jump into your mind? Is he really the wisest man who ever lived? When we think of Jesus, we often use words like "gentle," "kind," "compassionate," "loving," "caring," "powerful," etc. What about also using words like "smart," "intelligent," "brilliant," or "wise"? In his book *The Divine Conspiracy*, Dallas Willard asks,

Can we seriously imagine that Jesus could be *Lord* if he were not smart? If he were divine, would he be dumb? Or uninformed? Once you stop to think about it, how could he be what we take him to be in all other respects and not be the best-informed and most intelligent person of all, the smartest person who ever lived? (1997, 94).

Willard adds,

The biblical and continuing vision of Jesus was of one who made all of created reality and kept it working, literally 'holding it together' (Col. 1:17). And today we think people are smart who make light bulbs and computer chips and rockets out of 'stuff' already provided! He made 'the stuff'! (1997, 94).

When you think about what Willard said, it is at once hilarious and horrifying, humorous and humbling. How can we see Jesus as anything but the wisest man who ever lived? Yet, I fear, we rarely think of Him in those terms. When we see Him as just a nice man, we may like Him and may even imitate Him and try to be nice to others as well. But if we do not see Him as wise and all-knowing, we may not listen to what He says in other areas of our lives. Again, Willard says,

> Strangely, we seem prepared to learn how to live from almost anyone but him. We are ready to believe that the 'latest studies' have more to teach us about love and sex than he does, and that Louis Rukeyser knows more about finances. 'Dear Abby' can teach us more about how to get along with our family members and co-workers, and Carl Sagan is a better authority on the cosmos (1997, 55).

The New Testament describes Jesus as a man of wisdom. Consider the following examples from Jesus's life:

> And the child grew and became strong, *filled with wisdom*. And the favor of God was upon him. (Luke 2:40, emphasis mine)

> And coming to his hometown he taught them in their synagogue, so that they were astonished, and said, "*Where did this man get this wisdom* and these mighty works? (Matt 13:54, emphasis mine)

> And on the Sabbath he began to teach in the synagogue, and many who heard him were astonished, saying,

"Where did this man get these things? And *what is the wisdom* given to him? How are such mighty works done by His hands? Is not this the carpenter, the son of Mary and brother of James and Joses and Judas and Simon? And are not his sisters here with us?" And they took offense at him. (Mark 6:2–3, emphasis mine)

The queen of the South will rise up at the judgment with this generation and condemn it, for she came from the ends of the earth to hear the *wisdom of Solomon*, and behold, *something greater than Solomon is here*. (Matt 12:42, emphasis mine)

If Jesus could form the cosmos from nothing, could create the human circulatory system or a human mind which could formulate a means for sending a man to the moon, then He knows how I should live my life. He not only knows the Scriptures, but He also can help me to understand and apply them. "And beginning with Moses and all the Prophets, he interpreted to them in all the Scriptures the things concerning himself" (Luke 24:27, cf. 24:32).

Where did Jesus's wisdom come from? It may surprise you that I would ask that question. You may be thinking, "Of course He is wise, He is the divine Son of God (cf. John 20:28; 9:38), and the Holy Spirit assisted Him (Luke 3:22; 4:1–2)." However, we must also remember that He "emptied himself" when He became a human being (Phil. 2:7). As the divine Son of God, He was all-knowing. But in human flesh, He was not all-knowing. There was some sense in which He emptied Himself of knowledge. To be truly human like us, He could not have been born already knowing calculus or world geography. Ten minutes after His birth, the baby Jesus would have known what every other ten-minute-old child knows.

While on earth, Jesus said He did not know when He would come back to earth (Matt. 24:36). He said only the Father knew (though I think it is possible that Jesus knows now). Note that Luke tells us, "And Jesus increased in wisdom and in stature and in favor with God and man" (2:52). The fact that He increased in wisdom implies that He had degrees of knowledge in His earthly existence. He was not all-knowing as a human being.

So how did He become wise as a human being? In addition to guidance by the Holy Spirit, I notice other elements. First of all, Jesus regularly prayed to the Father. One example was the night before He chose the twelve (Luke 6:12–15). I would love to have been able to listen in on that conversation between the Father and the Son. Did they spend most of the night talking about the choices of Peter and Judas?

Secondly, He was raised by godly parents (Luke 2:39–41). Joseph and Mary would have played a critical role in helping the young Jesus rediscover who He really was. Luke 2:41–52, which we discussed in chapter 3, is where Jesus embraced His true identity. Heaven only knows the responsibility Mary and Joseph carried on their shoulders every day.

Thirdly, He sought advice from those who dedicated their lives to studying Scripture (Luke 2:46). During His three-day separation from His family, Jesus was in the temple with the teachers. (Have you ever wondered where He stayed during this period?) The text tells us He was not an unengaged bystander just passing the time, but He was listening and asking questions. Listening and asking questions are two of the most important pillars of learning. Great leaders are learners. They listen and ask, just like Jesus.

Finally, He developed a life habit of going to the synagogue for study of God's word (Luke 4:16). I cannot help but think of the people of Thessalonica who "received the word with all eagerness, examining the Scriptures daily to see if these things were so" (Acts 17:11). Scripture was imbedded in Jesus's consciousness such that when tempted by the devil, the word of God sprang forth: "It is written …" (Luke 4:4, 8). I think Mohler might say he had "convictional intelligence." His mental reflexes corresponded with biblical truth (2012, 34).

The Christian

"The Savior is sufficient and supreme." That is the theme phrase I use for the book of Colossians. Paul seems to be trying to counter some kind of false teaching that questioned the adequacy of Christ. He begins the book by praising the Colossians for their faith and love which are based on "hope laid up for you in heaven" (cf. Col. 1:3–5). They learned of this hope through the preaching of the word of truth by Epaphras. Having praised them, he then tells them that he is praying for them. He was specifically praying that they "may be filled the knowledge of his will in all spiritual wisdom and understanding" (Col. 1:9). Let us highlight three key words in this statement: "knowledge," "understanding," and "wisdom." "Knowledge" is information, "understanding" is insight into the meaning and significance of the information, and "wisdom" is knowing when, where, how, and why to apply the information. Paul wanted the Colossians to have spiritual knowledge, wisdom, and understanding, so they could live lives that please the Lord (Col. 1:10). Leaders must develop spiritual wisdom and understanding ("convictional intelligence"). They must learn to think like Jesus.

Decisions are part of leadership. Henry and Richard Blackaby make a very important statement about leadership and decision-making, saying,

> People who are unwilling or unable to make decisions are unlikely leadership candidates. ... People need the assurance that their leader is capable of making wise, timely decisions. The fear of making a wrong decision is the overriding impetus behind some people's leadership style. Such people become immobilized by their fear of making a mistake. It is true that all decisions have ramifications, and leaders must be prepared to accept the consequences of their decisions. Those without the fortitude to live with this reality should not take on leadership roles. (2001, 178)

Leaders in the church must be willing to make decisions and live with the consequences. We should also seek to make sure that those decisions are wise decisions. Peter F. Drucker states,

> Yet it's in the decision that everything comes together. That is the make or break point of the organization. Most of the other tasks that executives do, other people could do. But only executives can make the decisions.

And they either make decisions effectively or they render themselves ineffective (1990, 121).

The reality is that many in organizations must make decisions in order for the organization to be successful. Drucker's focus is on the leaders whose decisions impact the overall direction and policies for the organization. Those decisions must be effective. They need to be wise.

How do leaders make wise decisions? Let us consider again the influences in the life of Jesus: (1) prayer, (2) knowledge of God's word, and (3) input from others. We emphasized the importance of prayer earlier in this book, but it bears a reminder here. Leaders must be people of prayer. If Jesus felt it was important to talk to the Father before making decisions, then it would seem logical and right for us to do the same thing. Verbalizing our thoughts and needs to God helps us to sort out the situation in our minds, reminds us that we need help, and puts the problem/decision in the hands of the Creator of the universe.

We also noted that knowledge of God's word helped Jesus to know what to do when facing temptation. It can also help us to know what to do when we face decisions. We cannot have "convictional intelligence" or "mental reflexes corresponded with biblical truth" if we do not actually know biblical truth. Paul told Titus that elders were to hold fast the faithful word (Titus 1:9). They must do this so they "may be able to give instruction in sound doctrine and also to rebuke those who contradict it" (1:9). Elders should also be able to teach (1 Tim. 3:2). All of this requires knowledge of Scripture. James Estep Jr., in *Management Essentials for Christian Ministries*, identifies key questions that must be asked to make sure a decision is being made from a theologically informed perspective:

- Does the decision honor and glorify God?
- Is the decision consistent with God's revealed will in Scripture?
- Does the decision address the spiritual nature of humanity?
- Is its success based on a call to a maturing faithfulness?
- Does the decision affirm the nature of Christ's church and advance its mission? (2005, 226)

At various schools where I have taught, we have required memory verses in our Bible classes. This is often one of the least favorite parts of the class for students. I have seen many students who would ace a standard test and then fail a memory quiz. I found that few of them had memorized quotes, whether from Scripture or elsewhere, when they were in high school. They are not being trained in this kind of memory work. I have often talked to my students about how important memory work is. I would regularly use the temptation of Jesus as an example. We are often going to be in situations in which we have to make a decision about the right thing to do. I have frequently told my students that we will rarely be able to pull out our phones or look in a concordance to look up a verse that will tell us what to do. We will make decisions in the moment based on what is stored in our minds. If God's word is not stored in my mind, He may be left out of the decision. Spiritual leaders need to know the Bible.

Finally, wise leaders listen to others. Jesus listened to the religious leaders. He also frequently asked the apostles questions. I understand that these questions primarily had a teaching focus, but they also allowed Him to know what they were thinking and struggling with. Proverbs 11:14 states, "Where there is no guidance, a people falls, but in an abundance of counselors there is safety." It is interesting that in Acts 6 and in Acts 15, the apostles included the input of the members in their decision-making process (note 6:2–3; 15:22). Elders and deacons must not become detached from those they serve. True, they cannot make decisions by popular vote, but they also cannot serve those they do not know. They cannot know those that they do not listen to. There is a great deal of knowledge, wisdom, and experience in the average congregation, and leaders are unwise who do not take advantage of those resources.

We can gain much from how the apostles made a decision in the gathering recorded in Acts 15. The meeting described in this chapter focused on whether non-Jews needed to be circumcised. Here is what they did:

1. They identified the problem (15:6; they did not ignore it).
2. They gathered all the facts and allowed all sides to speak (15:5–7).
3. They gathered the wise (apostles, elders, James the brother of Jesus).
4. They listened to inspiration (inspired apostles, James quoting from Amos 9:11–12).
5. They involved the members (15:22).
6. They made a decision (15:19–22; they did not leave it unresolved).

7. They sent eyewitnesses to communicate the decision to others (15:22, 30; 16:4–5).
8. They wrote down their decision so they would have a record (15:23–29). Problems often arise when decisions are not recorded for the future. This is common in agreements between elders and preachers.

Our Administrative Council at Heritage Christian University reads through a different book together every semester. Some of these are devotional-type books, some are leadership books, and others are more academic in orientation. One book we found very valuable was *Institutional Intelligence*. The author, Gordon T. Smith, notes that leaders with institutional intelligence have a "threefold capacity to move from conversation to decision to action" (2017, 87). He highlights the following:

- They foster good conversation toward insight, wisdom, and creative solutions.
- They foster the capacity for closure—making the necessary decisions for organizational effectiveness.
- They have the system in place—the mechanisms —to move from having made the decision to actual implementation (Smith 2017, 87).

It is also worth adding that the decision made in Acts 6 concerning food for the Greek-speaking widows included assigning specific individuals to carry out the decisions. These same basic principles that are found in Acts 6 and 15 can work with many decisions made within congregations today.

It seems appropriate at this point to stop a moment and talk about elders and decision making. Some would notice that it looks like James made the decision in Acts 15. First of all, this is a somewhat unique setting, and James was a very unique person. He was the earthly brother of Jesus, and his opinion would have carried a great deal of weight. However, the text is also very clear that the apostles and elders were integral to the discussion and that these men and "the whole church" approved the decision and the reporting process. To use Acts 15 as evidence for one person serving as a dictator making decisions for one church or multiple churches would be very inappropriate. Elders clearly have authority. It is implied in the words "bishop" and "overseer" (*epískopos*). Biblically, this authority lies in the elder group, or eldership, not in the individual elder. Directives and guidelines to elders in Scripture are consistently addressed to a plurality of elders (cf. Acts 20:17–38). No elder should make a decision for the group. Individual elders may make decisions in specific areas of work but only by delegation from the elders as a group and in consistency with the decisions of the group. There should be no "lone ranger" elders acting arbitrarily, separate from the group. Individual elders have no more authority than any other older wise man in the congregation. They function, in some senses (not all), like Christian university boards. School boards have one employee, the president. As a school president, I answer to a board. They are my bosses. Yet only the group has authority over me. I do not have nineteen separate bosses who can give me nineteen separate orders. It is important for leadership groups, whether boards or elders, to work in unison. They will not always agree with each other; but they should always respect each other, give every elder a voice, make decisions in light of Scripture, and speak with a unified voice once the decision is made (like the Christians did in Acts 15).

It is also worth noting that Jesus often avoided rushing into a decision. Some scholars note that it may have been as much as a year and a half into Jesus's public ministry before He designated twelve of His disciples as apostles. When it came time to make the decision, He spent the night reflecting on it with the Father (Luke 6:12–13). There is also wisdom in considering the following words from Drucker: "The least effective decision makers are the ones who constantly make decisions. The effective ones make very few. They concentrate on the important decisions" (1990, 121). A logjam is created in congregations when elders must make every single decision and do not entrust deacons and other people of wisdom to make decisions where appropriate. The elders oversee the big picture decisions and policies that govern the congregation. It is not the best use of their time or membership abilities if they are deciding paint colors or where office personnel buy their paper clips. Think of the words of the apostles who said, "It is not right that we should give up preaching the word of God to serve tables" (Acts 6:2).

Conclusion

Americans were glued to their televisions during the heart of the COVID-19 crisis. This was not just because they had more time at home due to quarantines. It was because we wanted to know what was going on. We watched briefings from the president, governors, sheriff departments, and doctors. I actually assigned some of our administrative assistants at Heritage Christian University to watch certain official websites to keep us updated as information was changing on an hourly basis during certain periods of the crisis. When we made the decision to transfer all students to the distance learning format and asked our campus students to go home, we received some negative pushback from people (not too many). A few were very mean about it. The next day, when every other school did the same thing, the negative comments stopped. We want to trust that those leading us, those making major decisions, are doing so in a wise manner. Those of us who lead need to do our best to make the wisest decisions possible. We must do so even if others doubt our judgment. We must do so with the awareness that the one we ultimately answer to is God, not the naysayers and complainers (cf. 1 Peter 5:4). God deserves our best. He is worthy of wise decisions.

Discussion Questions

1. What does the phrase "apt to teach" mean?
2. Do you think being apt to teach is considered when the average congregation appoints elders? Why or why not?
3. What would you list as the number one mistake leaders make when making important decisions?

Homework

1. How many hours have you spent in the last

week in studying God's word outside of worship or a Bible class?

2. How many hours do you spend in the average week studying God's word outside of worship or Bible class?

3. Make a commitment to spend time in God's word every day this week.

8

COMPETENT

HE KNEW HIS STUFF

Introduction

GEORGE WASHINGTON, the first president of the United States, died on December 14, 1799 at the age of 67. He had spent five hours riding across his farm on December 12 and was caught out in stormy weather. When he returned home, he ate dinner in his wet clothes to keep his guest from waiting. Cold symptoms showed up the next day, but Washington insisted on going out anyway. He became seriously ill on the evening of the 13th, and doctors were called in the next morning. Ultimately, many believe a key factor in his death was the "treatment" he received from his doctors. They bled five pints of blood from his body (40 percent of the body's total), blistered his neck with poultices, and gave him laxatives. The actions that were supposed to save his life actually hastened his death. The experts who were supposed to help him to heal ended up causing him to die. Modern doctors cringe at the actions of the doctors who treated the former general and president.

Though primitive and dangerous by modern standards, these doctors were simply doing what they had been taught you should do. In spite of their good intentions, they were incompetent. A man, a family, and a nation paid the price (adapted from Metaxas 2015, 27). Good intentions are not enough when leading. Competence is a key to success. This is especially true for spiritual leaders. Eternal lives are at stake.

The Christ

William Cohen states,

> During World War II, the U.S. Army conducted a study to find out what soldiers thought about their leaders. ... They asked, 'What are the most important factors associated with good leadership?' The most frequent answer these researchers received was 'that the leader know his stuff' (2010, 25).

When you board a plane, you want a pilot that knows what he or she is doing. When you climb in a taxi, you want a driver who knows the city. People followed Jesus because He was a man of competency. He knew His stuff.

Jesus Knew Scripture

There is value in knowing something about reading, writing, and arithmetic. It can be beneficial to know something about farming, car repair, or money management. But if we know all of these things and do not know God's word, then we are ignorant of the most important information in the world. We live in a world in which people have little Bible knowledge. Note the following quote from an article written by Mohler on his website:

> While America's evangelical Christians are rightly concerned about the secular worldview's rejection of biblical Christianity, we ought to give some urgent attention to a problem much closer to home—biblical illiteracy in the church. This scandalous problem is our own, and it's up to us to fix it. Researchers George Gallup and Jim Castelli put the problem squarely: "Americans revere the Bible—but, by and large, they don't read it. And because they don't read it, they have become a nation of biblical illiterates" (Mohler 2016).

Lifeway research notes the following:

- "Only 20 percent of Americans say they've read the entire Bible at least once."
- Only 22 percent read their Bible every day.
- "A third of Americans never read the Bible on their own."
- 47 percent believe "the Bible is 100 percent accurate in all it teaches."
- 51 percent believe "the Bible was written for each person to interpret as he or she chooses."
- 45 percent believe there are many ways to get to heaven. (Braddy 2017)

If God's word can "make you wise for salvation" (2 Tim. 3:15), then we must know it. I am concerned when I see preachers and teachers who prefer to tell stories instead of teaching the word of God. While Jesus also told stories, He was definitely a man of the book. Jesus grew up with parents who modeled obedience to the law of Moses and took Him to Jerusalem to worship (Luke 2:39–43). He developed a habit early on of studying the Law. He was at the temple studying with the religious scholars at the age of twelve (Luke 2:46). Luke 4:16 tells us that going to the synagogue for study and worship was a habit in Jesus's life.

One out of every ten recorded words of Jesus is either a quote or an allusion to the Old Testament. J. M. Price notes the following concerning the recorded teachings of Jesus in the Gospels: "During his ministry he quoted from at least twenty of the books of the Old Testament" (1981, 16). Matthew's Gospel is a good place to note Jesus's knowledge of the Old Testament. It contains sixty-five quotes/allusions to the Old Testament, and forty-three of those are direct quotes. When Jesus was tempted in the wilderness by Satan, He responded by saying, "It is written" (Matt. 4:1–10). He quoted from Deuteronomy 8:3; 6:16; 6:13; and 10:20 respectively. Consider the following evidence of Jesus's knowledge of the Old Testament:

- Matthew 8:4—He is aware of the Law's teaching on showing oneself to the priest to be declared clean of leprosy (Lev. 13:49; 14:2ff).
- Matt. 12:3–5—He refers to David eating the consecrated bread in 1 Samuel 21:1-6.
- Matthew 15:4—He quotes Exodus 20:12; Deuteronomy 5:16; Exodus 21:17; Leviticus 20:9 (honor your father and mother).
- Matthew 15:8–9—He quotes Isaiah 29:13 (in vain they worship).

- Matthew 19:4—He quotes Genesis 1:27; 2:24 (they were male and female; leave father and mother).
- Matthew 19:8—He shows knowledge of Moses's teaching on divorce in Deuteronomy 24:1–4.
- Matthew 19:18–19—He quotes Exodus 20:12–16; Deuteronomy 5:16–20; Leviticus 19:18 as He mentions five of the ten commandments (to the rich young ruler).
- Matthew 21:5—He quotes Isaiah 62:11; Zechariah 9:9 (donkey's colt).
- Mention of Old Testament characters— Elsewhere He referred to Jonah (Matt. 12:39–40), the flood and Noah (Matt. 24:37–39; Luke 17:26–27), Abel (Matt. 23:35; Luke 11:51), Sodom (Matt. 11:24), Moses (Luke 24:27), and Abraham, Isaac, and Jacob (Matt. 8:11).

Jesus studied the word of God so He could teach the word of God. We must do the same. Luke said the students in Berea were "examining the Scriptures daily" (Acts 17:11). This example is so important to us at Heritage Christian University that we have named the Bible Class Series that we produce for churches the *Berean Study Series*. Are we like the Bereans? Are we searching the Scriptures?

Jesus Knew People

Maxwell notes, "If your desire is to be successful and make a positive impact on your world, you need the ability to understand others" (*Relationships* 2003, 7). There are many theories which seek to explain human beings and how they interact with each other. Systems theory originated in the 1940s. Scientists began to see life as a series of interacting systems. They identified certain features of those systems, such as reluctance to change. Generational theory highlighted characteristics of various generations and the repercussions of interaction between the generations. You could add to these such theories as Erick Erickson's personality development theory, Jean Piaget's cognitive development theory, or Lawrence Kohlberg's moral development theory.

What does this have to do with Jesus? The point is that human beings with numerous degrees have put a great deal of effort into trying to understand the human mind and human development. Jesus had no degree in sociology, psychology, or science. He didn't even have official training as a Jewish rabbi. What He did have was the knowledge that comes from being the Creator of human beings and from living among human beings as a human being. He made us. "In the beginning was the Word, and the Word was with God, and the Word was God. He was in the beginning with God. All things were made through him, and without him was not any thing made that was made" (John 1:1–3).

First of all, as Creator and by the assistance of the Holy Spirit, Jesus knew human thoughts and could see people from a distance. Consider the following:

> Now when he was in Jerusalem at the Passover Feast, many believed in his name when they saw the signs that he was doing. But Jesus on his part did not entrust himself to them, because he knew all people, and needed no one to bear witness about man, for he

himself knew what was in man (John 2:23–25, emphasis mine).

And behold, some people brought to him a paralytic, lying on a bed. And when Jesus saw their faith, he said to the paralytic, "Take heart, my son; your sins are forgiven." And behold, some of the scribes said to themselves, "This man is blaspheming." But Jesus, *knowing their thoughts*, said, "Why do you think evil in your hearts?" (Matt. 9:2–4, emphasis mine; cf. Luke 6:8; 11:17; Matt. 22:18)

Jesus saw Nathanael coming toward him and said of him, "Behold, an Israelite indeed, in whom there is no deceit!" Nathanael said to him, "How do you know me?" Jesus answered him, "Before Philip called you, when you were under the fig tree, I saw you." Nathanael answered him, "Rabbi, you are the Son of God! You are the King of Israel!" (John 1:47–49; cf. John 4:16–18)

And they put forward two, Joseph called Barsabbas, who was also called Justus, and Matthias. And they prayed and said, "*You, Lord, who know the hearts of all,* show which one of these two you have chosen to take the place in this ministry and apostleship from which Judas turned aside to go to his own place." And they cast lots for them, and the lot fell on Matthias, and he was numbered with the eleven apostles. (Acts 1:23–26, emphasis mine)

Jesus also understood human beings because He became one (John 1:14). The Hebrew writer stressed that the humanity of Jesus helped to make Him the great High Priest:

> Therefore he had to be made like his brothers in every respect, so that he might become a merciful and faithful high priest in the service of God, to make propitiation for the sins of the people. For because he himself has suffered when tempted, he is able to help those who are being tempted (Heb. 2:17–18).

He was born as a human baby. As such, He had to be cared for (Luke 2:7), He had to be protected (Matt. 2:13–15), and He had to go through a process of growth and maturity (Luke 2:40, 52). He got weary, thirsty, and hungry (John 4:6–8). There were times He needed sleep (Matt. 8:24). He dealt with ridicule, disappointment, and failure. He experienced death and heartbreak. He felt emotions like compassion (Matt. 14:14), love (John 11:5), anger (Mark 3:5), joy (Luke 10:21), and grief (Matt. 26:37–38). He even experienced astonishment (Matt. 8:10; Mark 6:6) and dread (John 11:33; 12:27). He could relate to the experiences of those He taught (Heb. 4:15). Jesus knew people because He created them and became one of them. You might say He knew His students inside and out. Jesus had an intimate knowledge of those He taught that allowed Him to respond to their needs and problems.

Jesus Knew Teaching

Teaching is not easy. Students are at different stages of mental, physical, and spiritual development. There are gender, ethnic, generational, and socio-economic differences between students. There are language barriers and differences in learning styles. In a typical class at Heritage Christian University, I might have students who are in their late teens, and I might have elders who are in their 70s. I might have students from Albania, India, Russia, Vietnam, the Netherlands, or the United Arab Immigrants, in addition to students from across the United States. I have students who are sitting in the classroom while others join the class online (and still others watch a recording of the class when they get off from work or first thing in the morning after they wake up). I cannot have just one approach to teaching because I do not have just one type of student.

Teaching did not wait until the twenty-first century to become challenging. It had its own challenges in the first century as well. Jesus lived in a world in which three languages had influence: Greek, Aramaic, and, to a lesser degree, Hebrew. People around Jerusalem tended to speak Aramaic. People around Galilee mostly spoke Greek. Jesus had to teach in both of these environments. When He spoke, He might on one occasion be speaking to the people around Galilee, who were tradespeople and fishermen with little formal education outside of the synagogues. On another day, He might be speaking to Scribes and Pharisees, who had devoted their lives to a study of the law of Moses. On other occasions, He spoke to Samaritans, who rejected all but the first five books of the Old Testament and had set up their own place and means of worship at Mount Gerizim. Thus, Christ needed incredible competence as a teacher to be able to reach people in all of these settings.

Are some teachers more interesting than others? I think

we would all recognize that there are. There are teachers who know a lot of information about their subject, but you would rather watch paint dry than listen to them. Then there are some teachers who have this special ability to connect with people. Jesus was such a teacher. He knew the art of teaching.

Investigation of the teaching and leadership of Jesus shows that He used a variety of methods. Sometimes He used verbal instruction (Mark 1:21–22). Even this had variety in it. He might use challenging statements (cf. Matt. 5:3–4), ask a thought-provoking question (cf. Matt. 16:13–15), paint a word picture (Matt. 5:6), tell a story (Matt. 13:3–9), or use an object lesson (Mark 9:36–37).

He used role play in His teaching. In John 6 He asked Philip where they should buy bread to feed the large crowd that had come to hear Him preach. Jesus was not asking this because He did not know where to buy food. It was a teaching method (cf. John 6:6). Jesus already knew what He was going to do. He had the situation completely under control. He wanted to test Philip by putting him in the position of considering how he might handle the situation. Philip did not have to feed the people, but he did have to simulate doing so and consider in the process how much faith he had in Christ.

Jesus also used experiential learning. In Luke 10:1–6, we find Jesus training seventy of His disciples. He gave them guidance on how to conduct themselves and then sent them out in pairs. In Luke 10:17–21 we find the seventy returning and reporting to Jesus what happened, with Jesus giving them feedback. This type of experiential learning is similar to what can be seen when a Sunday morning teacher talks about loving others and then takes his or her class to the nursing home after morning worship services. Jesus did this by taking His apostles everywhere He went for three years. They learned what it meant to follow in Jesus's footsteps by literally walking in His footsteps.

The message of the examples above is that Jesus knew the craft of teaching. He used many different teaching styles. His knowledge of Scripture and people and the art of teaching allowed Him to take these different teaching techniques and adapt them to the needs of His students and the teaching situation so He could connect the word of God to people's lives.

He Knew Hard Work

It is interesting that Jesus worked as a carpenter for several years before working as a preacher. He likely had calloused hands. His life as a carpenter would have taught Him how to work with the public and how to work hard. If He was not willing to work, He would not last long as a carpenter. Those lessons would have carried over into His public ministry. He rose early in the morning to pray after a long day of work the day before (cf. Luke 4:40–44; Mark 1:35). He took time to have a noontime spiritual conversation with a Samaritan woman when He was tired, thirsty, and hungry (cf. John 4:6). The word translated as "wearied" in John 4 refers to a weariness that comes from hard labor to the point of exhaustion (Mounce 2006, 386). Jesus entertained visitors at night (John 3:1–21). I think of the words of John 9, "We must work the works of him who sent me while it is day; night is coming, when no one can work" (John 9:4). Jesus was "all in." He was willing to lay down His life for His followers (John 10:11). When you are committed enough to a cause or a group that you would die for it, no one will have to motivate you to work hard for it!

The Christian

As we wrestle with the competency of Jesus, let me share two principles that guide my life. The first is "Do not let anyone outwork you." I have often told my students, "You cannot change the world lying in bed." You can tell the maturity of students by how late they stay up and how early they get up (unless, of course, they work the night shift and need to sleep in the day). When I see someone who stays up at night playing games and watching TV, and then will not get up and go to work or class on time the next day, I see a child, not an adult. You cannot change the world lying in bed! Paul stressed the importance of work in his second letter to the Thessalonians: "For even when we were with you, we would give you this command: If anyone is not willing to work, let him not eat. For we hear that some among you walk in idleness, not busy at work, but busybodies" (2 Thess. 3:10–11). We all understand there are exceptions to this, such as those who are physically unable, but Paul's message is clear. "If anyone does not work, neither shall he eat." This should apply even more so to spiritual leaders. People do not respect laziness. They will look down on our ministry and our leadership if we are lazy. We cannot expect them to work if we are not willing to. We should view no job as below us and no hour of the day as off-limits. We must lead by an example of hard work.

In addition, we need to remember who is working against us. Stott tells the story of Hugh Latimer, who preached "The Sermon of the Plough" at Saint Paul's

Cathedral on January 18, 1548. In that sermon, Latimer talked about the one he considered to be the most diligent preacher in all of England. Who did he say it was? The devil (Stott 1982, 26–27). I remember a favorite phrase my father would use when I was a boy and would try to resist going with him to a Bible study with a non-Christian. He said, "Son, it's a war out there, and the devil never takes a day off!" Consider the words of Paul to servants at Colossae who were Christians: "Whatever you do, work heartily, as for the Lord and not for men, knowing that from the Lord you will receive the inheritance as your reward. You are serving the Lord Christ" (Col. 3:23–24; cf. 2 Cor. 11:23). As church leaders, we are servants of God and the church. Both deserve our best.

A second principle that guides my life is "Never stop learning." Those words are printed on a yellow sign that is attached to a 100-plus-year-old school slate that hangs in my office. I have been teaching people about Jesus since I was ten years old. I have spent a lifetime teaching in local congregations, for lectureships, for workshops, and on college campuses. Still, most every day I learn something new. To function as a professor in today's world, I have had to learn more computer programs, apps, websites, digital technologies, teaching platforms, and social media platforms than I can count. I can never stop learning and must constantly try new things. I think of C. Wayne Kilpatrick. Wayne is in his seventies and has taught at Heritage Christian University for over forty years. I recently looked in our newest technology classroom and saw him teaching. He has had to learn amazing new technology, and he has had to learn how to teach a class with both in-classroom students and distance learning students. I was struck with all the adjustments he has had to make as a teacher over the years. The circumstances surrounding COVID-19 have thrust even more changes on him. It has not always come easily for him, but I greatly appreciate the fact that he is trying.

Leaders must be lifetime learners. Let me be frank for a moment and talk about a pet peeve. Now let me begin by saying that I understand that I am biased because I came from a preaching background. I have never served as an elder (though I have served as a deacon). Having said that, here is my frustration. Congregations put a great deal of emphasis on their preachers and youth ministers being trained but put little emphasis on their elders and deacons being trained. Many churches require at least a two-year degree from a preaching school and churches 150 or more in membership frequently require a four-year bachelor's degree in Bible from an accredited institution. There are large congregations that want their preacher to have an accredited master's degree. I see preachers and youth ministers go to lectureships and workshops on at least a yearly basis to help them grow as leaders and servants of God. I also see them work under elders and with deacons who are doing nothing to train and grow as leaders. They read no books, watch no training videos, listen to no audio books, attend no lectureships or workshops, do no in-congregation training classes or seminars, and have no conversations with elders or deacons from other congregations so they can learn and grow as leaders. Maybe we should not be surprised that there is a leadership problem in the church.

The most important knowledge for spiritual leaders to have is knowledge of God's word. Paul said of an elder, "He must hold firm to the trustworthy word as taught, so that he may be able to give instruction in sound doctrine and also to rebuke those who contradict it" (Titus 1:9). Do we stress knowledge of God's word as much as we stress business ability when appointing elders? I have known of many godly elders and elderships with deep and insightful knowledge of God's word. I have also seen elderships who know little of God's word and rely on their preacher to know the Bible for them. As a result of this, it is all too easy for preachers to lead entire congregations astray. Spiritual leaders cannot lead God's people toward God's goals unless they know God's will and word. Spiritual leaders must be competent leaders. God, and God's people deserve our best. Competent leaders never stop learning!

Conclusion

We can all remember a junior high math teacher, a high school English teacher, or a college professor that everyone wanted for a teacher. I remember Mr. Huccaby. He was my high school chemistry teacher. I am sure there were other teachers who knew as much chemistry as he did. I also know that chemistry was not my favorite subject. Yet I enjoyed Mr. Huccaby's class. He knew his stuff. He knew chemistry, and he seemed to genuinely enjoy teaching chemistry. He had this ability to relate to us and to make chemistry fun for us. He made us laugh. We also had this feeling that he genuinely liked us. We voted him our favorite teacher my senior year. When leaders know their content, their craft, and their people, life changing relationships happen.

Discussion Questions

1. What are three areas in which the typical leader needs to grow and mature?
2. Why might preachers be expected to educate themselves, yet elders, deacons, and Bible class teachers are often not expected to do so? Are these reasons valid?
3. Make a list of specific resources that are available to you in your area to grow as a leader (workshops, conferences, experts you can bring in to speak to the congregation, books, videos, websites, etc.). Be specific.

Homework

1. Read or watch one resource on leadership this week, and list three things you learned.
2. Contact one leader you respect and ask that person to share two or three leadership principles that he or she lives by.

9

COURAGEOUSLY CALM
HE COULD SLEEP IN THE STORMS

Introduction

A FORMER MAJOR general in the U.S. Air Force Reserve, William Cohen, states, "There is no way to lead from the rear in combat, and there is no way to lead from the rear in corporate life. You have to be 'up front,' where the action is" (2010, 89). He goes on to say, "Employees don't follow leaders who spend all their time behind desks" (Cohen 2010, 90). I recently read Winston Groom's book *The Generals*, which focuses on Generals Patton, MacArthur, and Marshall. I was struck with how often they put themselves in harm's way. Cohen confirms that reputation for Patton and MacArthur in particular. He credits Patton with saying, "If you want an army to fight and risk death, you've got to get up there and lead it. An army is like spaghetti. You can't push a piece of spaghetti, you've got to pull it" (2010, 89). Napoleon Bonaparte was known for telling his commanders to "always march toward the sounds of the guns" (Cohen 2010, 94).

Great military leaders have this incredible ability to remain calm and make critical decisions as death and fire rains down around them. We must remember that, as spiritual leaders, we are engaged in a great battle with evil forces from beyond this earthly realm (cf. Eph. 6:10–20). Peter tells us that we fight "a roaring lion, seeking someone to devour" (1 Peter 5:8). To be a leader is to be at the front. To be at the front is to face the guns and the claws. It requires courageous calm. Let us consider the courageous calm of Jesus.

The Christ

Jesus faced countless challenging situations: interruptions (Mark 2:1–5), questions (Mark 10:17–22), attacks (Matt. 19:1–12), false accusations (Matt. 26:59–64), and rejection (John 6:60–71). While these situations were no doubt painful, He did not let them deter Him from His mission. Jesus was able to calmly handle each of these situations. One example found in Luke 5 might serve to illustrate Jesus's ability to remain calm in difficult situations.

A Story

Luke 5:17 and following shows Jesus teaching. As He did so, He faced at least two problems. The first problem was *corruption*. Jesus had stalkers. Pharisees and teachers of the law were listening to Jesus teach. They were frequently there to find fault, not to learn (cf. Luke 6:7). I can think of times in local congregations and in university classrooms in which there were those in the audience who were not there to learn; they were there to nitpick everything I said and find something wrong. It is not a fun place to be. Jesus felt it all the time. He had it much worse. His stalkers wanted to kill Him.

People have different ways of dealing with stress. Physical exercise has frequently been one of my ways of destressing. For several years, I destressed and tried to take care of myself physically by working out at a local boxing gym. Dr. Hines, a dentist in Columbia, Tennessee, started this gym to get at-risk kids off the streets. One of his rules was that "you fight in the ring with gloves, not on the streets." He helped countless young men and women to avoid destructive paths. Sparing sessions were part of the regular routine in the gym. What was interesting to me was that people would get in the ring and then spend the whole round running away. They would be so afraid of being hit that they would not throw punches themselves. This always puzzled me. Not wanting to be punched is a pretty wise thing, and I highly recommend it. However, if that is your desire, do not get in a boxing ring. Boxing rings are for punching. Wrestling mats are for grappling. Football fields are for tackling. Hockey rinks are for all of the above. The point is that if you cannot take a punch, a hold, a block, a tackle, or a cross check, don't get into the ring or onto the mat, field, or rink. Likewise, spiritual leaders need to understand that they are not officers at a country club; they are commanders in a spiritual army. Being punched, stabbed, targeted, and shot at is just part of the territory. I was never shocked when someone punched me in the nose in a boxing ring. That is what I expected when I climbed in. No matter how hard we try, there will be people who do not like us. Some will even try to hurt us. Spiritual leaders will get punched. It is just part of the territory. The way we "fight back," as spiritual leaders, is by staying focused on God's mission and the work He has given us to do, loving like Jesus, and being people of integrity. Peter challenged his readers to have "a good conscience, so that, when you are slandered, those who revile your good behavior in Christ may be put to shame" (1 Peter 3:16).

A second problem Jesus faced in Luke 5 was *interruption*. Jesus taught in many places: synagogues, fields, hillsides, and homes. Jesus was teaching in a home in the story we are considering in this chapter. There were so many people in the house that no one else could get in. Four friends had heard that a miracle worker was in town. With hearts full of hope, they had loaded a mutual friend onto a pallet and carried him to the healer. When they arrived, they were no doubt heartbroken to learn that there was no room. This did not stop them.

First-century Jewish homes were often flat-roofed with a set of stairs that went up the side of the house to the roof. The roofs were often made by placing beams across the width of the building and then smaller beams (in the opposite direction), with brush, earth, and clay on top of that. It was not uncommon for grass to sprout on the roof once rain started falling on it. This would only serve to strengthen the structure. Imagine yourself in that room. Everyone is trying to be quiet to hear Jesus. You begin to hear sounds coming from the roof. Digging sounds grow louder and louder and dust and dirt begin to cascade into the room. Eventually Jesus has to stop as everyone looks at the ceiling. Light appears and beams are broken or removed. Then, to everyone's amazement, a body is lowered down into the room.

Now, here is where we see Jesus's calm. Think of all of

the things He could have focused on. He could have been frustrated with the fact His message was interrupted. In Luke 4:18, 43, He had said that He came to earth to preach. He was no doubt sharing important information when the friends interrupted His message. Jesus could also have focused on the *destruction*. Remember that a roof was destroyed in someone's home. It was likely the home of a friend or at least someone with whom He was acquainted. He could have been upset by the fact that this family now had a hole through which the rain could fall. These were not the things that Jesus focused on. The text says that He saw their faith (Luke 5:20). He did not see corruption, interruption, or destruction; He saw four friends who loved their friend so much and believed in Jesus so much that they were willing to tear a house down to get the two together.

His faith-focused attitude stands in stark contrast to the fault-finding attitude of the religious leaders we see highlighted in Luke 5 and 6. How we handle situations will often be impacted by our attitudes. It is important to notice that conflict and difficulties did not cause Jesus to lose His compassion or His composure. Difficult times and attacks from the stalkers can cause us to become angry and calloused, and we can forget to notice the hurting people around us who need our love and help. Difficult times can also cause us to become discouraged and back down. When the religious leaders accused Jesus of doing what only God can do, He did not back down. He spoke up: "Which is easier, to say, 'Your sins are forgiven you,' or to say, 'Rise and walk'?" (Luke 5:23). His point was that they are both things that only God can do. He did not shy away from the truth of who He was and is. We often focus on the fact that Jesus said little at His trial. We forget that when slapped, He confronted the one who struck Him, asking, "If what I said is wrong, bear witness about the wrong; but if what I said is right, why do you strike Me?" (John 18:23). Even in the face of death, Jesus was courageously calm.

A Storm

There is no better example of Jesus's calm attitude than when He faced the raging Sea of Galilee. Years ago, a guest preacher at the Christian Chapel church of Christ in Hatley, Mississippi, asked the question, "Can you sleep when the wind blows?" Luke 8 tells us that Jesus could. The sea of Galilee is down in a bowl roughly thirteen miles long and seven miles wide. While visiting there many years ago, I was struck by the towering cliff on the eastern side of the lake. The cliff rises 1,000 feet on that side. Rolling hills serve as the boundary on the western side. Warm air from off the Mediterranean Sea to the west blows towards Galilee and mixes with cooler air in the hills. This mixture creates violent storms that fishermen down in the Galilean bowl cannot see until the storms are on top of them. To be on the lake during one of those storms would be something like being a small Hershey's kiss down in cake mix in my mother's mixing bowl while the mixer was spinning.

Jesus and the apostles were caught in such a storm. It was so bad that the apostles thought they were going to die (Luke 8:24). Think about what was going on here. These were fishermen. They had spent their lives on the water. When the sailors and seasoned fisherman are afraid of a storm on the water, I am scared to death. What was Jesus doing in the midst of all of this? He was sleeping. In the midst of a swirling vortex of death, Jesus slept! This is a vivid example of how Jesus faced life in general. He faced life with a peace and calm that others could only marvel at.

The Secrets

What were the secrets to His success? Why was Jesus able to remain so calm? There are five characteristics which might answer this question.

First of all, Jesus was prepared. Preparation is a first key to calm. Jesus spent thirty years studying Scripture and learning people before He encountered these situations. He knew people, and He knew God's word, and they became components of calm.

Second of all, Jesus had a clear understanding of His mission. We noted earlier that Jesus had a clear sense of what He was here to do. Thus, He was better able to handle problems and difficulties. Jesus did come to preach (Luke 4:43), but He ultimately came to save people (Luke 19:10). He wanted people to believe in Him. Preaching was a means to an end, not the end itself. The entrance of the five friends may have interrupted His sermon, but it actually accelerated His goal of creating faith. Jesus was not worried about the storm on Galilee in part because His mission required a death on a cross, not a boat. Calm grows out of a clear sense of mission.

Third, Jesus had a clear sense of who He was and a total absence of pride. His sense of identity and humility allowed Him to calmly react to situations. Jesus was not trying to win favor or boost His ego. He simply tried to do the right thing and fulfill His mission.

Fourth, Jesus understood His limitations. This may seem strange to say of Jesus. Jesus knew that He would not force anyone to believe, and therefore some people would not listen. It did not shock Him or cause Him to lose control when someone disagreed or confronted Him. Leaders who expect everyone to follow are destined for failure.

Most of all, Jesus placed His trust in the Father. Remember His words to the apostles: "Where is your faith?" (Luke 8:25). Jesus knew that He was not alone in the boat during that storm. He was comfortable in His relationship with the Father. He knew God would take care of Him.

There are other principles which you might have identified. These are just a few that I noted. To sum up, remember the words of Thomas à Kempis: "Keep yourself first in peace, and then you shall be able to pacify others" (à Kempis 1958, 67). In other words, calm exteriors come from calm interiors and spread calmness to others. Jesus had an inner peace which allowed Him to remain calm in any situation and to lead others through the storms of life.

The Christian

Can we sleep when the wind blows? Do we have peace when the storms of life swirl around us? Many of us live our lives in constant turmoil. We are like a live hand grenade which already has the pin pulled. We are just waiting to "go off." Do we have the five elements in our lives that Jesus had in His?

What about our preparation? If one is well prepared, he or she will not be as disturbed by corruption, interruption, or destruction. It is uncertainty that comes with a lack of preparedness that often leads to avalanches of doubt, fear, and overreaction.

Do we have a sense of purpose? A sense of purpose

gives leaders confidence and direction as they approach each circumstance. Often, unexpected interruptions and problems provide the greatest opportunities. The teenager who interrupts the high school class just might become a Peter who leads thousands to Christ, if we will just remain calm.

What about our sense of identity and humility? A lack of identity can cause us to be crowd-pleasers. Pride can cause us to be defensive, lash out, and lose control. We may overreact out of a lack of confidence or too much pride. It is interesting how often these two things are very closely connected.

Do we understand our limitations? We need to if we are going to be successful leaders. We should accept that we will not please everyone, and some may disagree with us. Once we accept this, apprehension is often replaced with calm.

Finally, how strong is our trust in our Creator? I cannot help but think of the reaction of the apostles when Jesus calmed the storm. "Who then is this, that even the wind and the sea obey him?" (Mark 4:41). They doubted because they did not know who was in the boat with them. What about us? Peter said, "Peace to all of you who are in Christ" (1 Peter 5:14). Have you ever noticed how many New Testament books end with a similar prayer (2 John 3; 3 John 15; letters of Paul, etc.). I think the New Testament writers are trying to tell us something.

It's a Whole New World

In his book *Canoeing the Mountains*, Tod Bolsinger tells the story of Meriwether Lewis and William Clark's expedition to explore the newly acquired Louisiana Purchase.

Explorers had been searching for over 300 years for a water route that would connect the Pacific Ocean to the Mississippi River. When Meriwether Lewis arrived at the continental divide after fifteen months of travel, he and his team were carrying canoes. It had been assumed for hundreds of years that land west of the continental divide was the same as land east of the continental divide. They expected to top a hill and find a gentle slope and a nice easy water route to the Pacific Ocean. Instead, they found miles and miles of the Rocky Mountains as far as the eyes could see. As they moved forward, they were traveling into uncharted territory, and their canoes were useless (Bolsinger 2015, 24–27). Bolsinger states,

> As he stepped off the map into uncharted territory, Meriwether Lewis discovered that what was in front of him was nothing like what was behind him, and that what had brought him to the this point in the journey would take him no farther. Lewis faced a daunting decision: What would he do now? Lewis and Clark and their Corps of Discovery were looking for a water route, but now they had run out of water. *How do you canoe over mountains?* You don't. If you want to continue forward, you change. You adapt. (2015, 34)

The author highlighted the current state of Christianity and how it is very different from the past. The Christian world that lies in front of us is not like what lies behind us, and we must be prepared to put aside our canoes and adapt.

What is interesting about Bolsinger's message is that it was written in 2015, five years before the earthshaking events of 2020. Throughout 2020, I kept hearing people talk about "when things get back to normal." The fact is that we crossed a cultural continental divide, and there is no going back. Canoes will not work where we are going. The gospel is still the same, but most everything else is different. Some of the changes had been desperately needed. Racism and bigotry must end. Christian leaders have been silent for far too long. Other changes were unwelcome. The pandemic, rioting in the streets, and attacks against law enforcement personnel who put their lives on the line are a few examples of the latter. We fought over masks or no masks, whether virtual gatherings were real gatherings, and how we felt about online giving. If we thought things were going back to the way they used to be, we were naïve. Here is my point. We have moved off the cultural map. Leadership in this uncharted territory is going to be even more important. It will require leaders with courageous calm, with the fortitude to stick to the truth of God's word, and a willingness to consider new ways of sharing the gospel and connecting to people. Do we have the courage to put aside our canoes while keeping our compasses?

Conclusion

Have you ever noticed how a child is able to handle a storm? When the wind batters the windows and the rain pummels the roof, the child will awaken in startled fear, crawl into bed with his or her parents, and drop off to sleep. What is the difference? It is the same house in the same storm with the same rattling windows. The difference is that the child is in the arms of mom and dad. The child's calm comes from trust in his or her parents. Maybe we would handle the pressures of leadership better if we trusted the arms of our Father. Years after the events of Luke 8, Peter was preparing to die. He had been sentenced by Herod to be executed the next morning. When the angel arrived to release him from his cell, Peter was sound asleep (Acts 12:7). In fact, the text says that the angel had to strike him to wake him up. He had learned to sleep in his storm. May we do the same.

Discussion Questions

1. Give examples of times in the past in which God delivered and provided for you or your congregation.
2. How can remembering past deliverance help us to face future difficulties?
3. How can difficulties in the past impact how we view things in the present? (Consider Acts 12.)
4. If you were writing this chapter, what would you list as key principles that help leaders to remain courageous and calm?

Homework

1. Read the beginning and end of the New Testament letters and note how many refer to peace.
2. Do a concordance search for the word "peace" in the New Testament. Scan through several of the passages and list your observations.

10

COACH (PART 1)

HE TRAINED THE NEXT GENERATION

Introduction

FORMER BRITISH PRIME Minister Winston Churchill led his nation through one of its most tumultuous times during World War II. He made the following insightful statement:

There is a special moment when a person is figuratively tapped on the shoulder and offered the chance to do a very special thing, unique to him and fitted to his talents; what a tragedy if that moment finds him unprepared or unqualified for the work which would have been his finest hour (quoted in Gangel 1997, 250).

The Christ

Jesus took leadership development very seriously. I have been blessed by using *The Maxwell Leadership Bible*. The copy I have has the New King James Version of the biblical text. Maxwell has taken excerpts and highlights from his books on leadership and has inserted them into relevant sections of the Bible. He observes, "The Son of God invested the vast majority of His time with twelve, not twelve hundred. Jesus practiced the axiom: More time with less people equals greater kingdom impact" (2007, 1265).

Those who came to hear Jesus speak had many different levels of commitment. You might think of these levels as like the rings on a target. The outer ring would be the crowds of people who came to Jesus for teaching and healing. Many of these had a low level of commitment (cf. John 6:26–27). In the next ring, you have the converts who came to believe that Jesus was the Christ (John 11:45; 12:11). Still further toward the center of the target, you have those disciples who committed themselves to traveling with Jesus to be further molded and trained by Him (like the seventy in Luke 10:1). Finally, you have the bull's eye, the apostles who were handpicked by Jesus to be eyewitnesses of His life, death, and resurrection and to tell what they saw in Jerusalem, Judea, Samaria, and the remotest parts of the earth (cf. Luke 6:12–15; Acts 1:8). As we continue our thoughts, I want to focus on the final two groups, the traveling disciples and the apostles.

Jesus Put the Right People on the Bus

In his book *Good to Great*, Collins highlights what his research revealed are the differences between good companies and great companies. He states,

> The executives who ignited the transformations from good to great did not first figure out where to drive the bus and then get people to take it there. No, they *first* got

the right people on the bus (and the wrong people off the bus) and *then* figured out where to drive it (Collins 2001, 41).

I saw my father following this principle as well. During his career, he served as plant manager for Gates Polyflex in Elizabethtown, Kentucky; served as senior vice president of the National Management Association (made up of leaders from across the country); and served as chairman of the Kentucky State School Board. One story concerning my dad may serve to illustrate the concept under consideration.

I grew up near Fort Knox military base, so I worshiped with several soldiers over the years. (By the way, I thank God for those who are willing to put their lives on the line to defend us!) One young man, who had finished his military career, got a job at Gates through a temp agency. When that job ran out, my dad and his team created a position, which involved combining several part-time jobs, and hired the young man full-time. When we were talking one day, Dad explained to me why they did it. He said, "When you find good people, don't let them walk out the door. If you do, your competitors will hire them. If you don't have a job, create one. You want good people on your team." Getting the right people "on the bus" and into the right seats is one of the most important responsibilities of leaders. I made it one of my top priorities when I became president of Heritage Christian University.

As we think of the rings of commitment that I referred to above, Jesus gave all who were willing the opportunity to be on the believing and discipling bus. Still, even within the wider discipling group, there seem to have been some given special training and ministry roles. An example would be the seventy that He sent out in Luke 10:1. The twelve, on the other hand, were handpicked to be on the apostle bus. Here are a few things I noticed concerning whom He chose to be on that bus.

Let us begin by just noticing some general things. He chose people He knew or who came from near where He grew up. Eleven of the twelve were from around Galilee (Cana, Bethsaida, Capernaum). There is a very good chance that two of them were His first cousins (James and John).

He had some diversity in the group. You did have several fishermen, but you also had a tax collector, a religious zealot, and someone who grew up near Jerusalem (two or three days' walk from the other apostles). We need to be careful not to read too much into this. We should not decide, for example, that we must have twelve elders, and eleven need to live near each other. Maybe the reason He primarily chose people from Galilee was that their main job was be eyewitnesses to His life, and those around Galilee had more exposure. It may have provided opportunities for them to encounter Him.

While being careful not to stretch Jesus's example too far, there are a few things that are worth noting. First of all, He seems to have waited a little while before choosing the twelve. Most scholars think that He waited at least a year after His public ministry began. This would have allowed Him time to get to know them.

Second, He prayed about the decision. In fact, Luke tells us that He prayed all night (Luke 6:12). I would love to have been a fly on a rock and have been able to listen to that prayer (especially the discussion of Peter). Why Judas?

Ultimately, Jesus will have to answer that question definitively for us. I cannot help but think that God needed someone who would pave the way to the cross, and the heart of Judas made him a prime candidate. God uses even those who do evil to carry out His will (cf. Pharaoh).

Third, He does not seem to have cared about position or power. Matthew, because of his position as a tax collector, would have had money and some influence in Roman circles. Peter, Andrew, James, and John had what might be described today as a middle-class fishing business. They had multiple boats and hired helpers (Luke 5:7; Mark 1:20). Outside of this, there was no real power or influence in the group (Acts 4:13). There seem to have been no wealthy landowners, priests, or kings.

Finally, I note that Jesus's focus seems to have been on the hearts of those whom He chose. A key passage that stands out to me is Acts 1:24–25: "And they prayed and said, 'You, Lord, who know the hearts of all, show which one of these two you have chosen to take the place in this ministry and apostleship from which Judas turned aside to go to his own place.'" This request tells me that either the apostles knew the heart of an apostle matters, or they knew that right hearts were important to Jesus, or maybe they knew both were true. Either way, they asked Jesus to examine the hearts of Joseph and Matthias. I am reminded of the words of 1 Samuel 16:7:

> But the LORD said to Samuel, 'Do not look on his appearance or on the height of his stature, because I have rejected him. For the LORD sees not as man sees: man looks on the outward appearance, but the LORD looks on the heart.'

Jesus Prepared the Passengers

It is not enough to get the right people on the leadership bus. We must prepare them for the seats they will occupy. Jesus trained the twelve both before and after they were chosen. The Holy Spirit continued to train them after Jesus went back to heaven (cf. John 14:26; 16:13). Jesus did four things to prepare these leaders. He educated them, involved them, evaluated them, and encouraged them. We will focus on one of those in this lesson and the others in the next.

He Began by Educating Them

They heard Him preach and teach before they were given jobs to do. He taught them in many different ways: lecture (Matt. 5:1), parables (Matt. 13:36), discussion questions (Mark 8:27–29), role play (John 6:5–6), etc. His training involved both discipleship and leadership training. I describe discipleship as the process of shaping people into the likeness of Christ. Eric Geiger and Kevin Peck make an interesting observation in their book *Designed to Lead*:

> Jesus did not divorce leadership development from discipleship. As He invested in the Twelve, He continually 'discipled' them while simultaneously developing them to be leaders. While it may be helpful to view leadership development as advanced discipleship or as a subset of discipleship, it is detrimental to view leadership development as distinct from discipleship (2016, 153).

I think of a comment my friend and former coworker Stan Mitchell made about the priority of discipleship in his book *Equipping the Saints for the Ministry*. He stated, "No equipment without commitment" (Mitchell 2010, 25). Before Christians can be equipped for ministry, they must be committed disciples of Jesus. Remember that the apostles were chosen from a wider group of disciples who traveled with Jesus (cf. Luke 6:13; Acts 1:21–22). They heard Jesus's teaching on the nature of God's kingdom and what it means to live as citizens of that kingdom (cf. Matt. 5–7; Luke 6; 13). They also received specific training about what it means to be spiritual leaders (cf. Matt. 20:20–28). God's leaders must know both how to live like Christ (discipleship) and how to lead like Christ (leadership).

The Christian

Now let us think about how this applies to us. As we think about the example of Jesus, we should be reminded that we need to believe in and see the best in people. Jesus saw what Peter could become, not what he was. Our goal as Christians should be to build people up and not tear them down (cf. Eph. 4:29–32). Leaders have a special responsibility to equip and train workers for Christ and to help shape them into the image of the Savior (Eph. 4:11–16). In his book *Developing the Leaders Around You*, Maxwell states, "Most people believe that each new generation of leaders is born rather than developed. They think that new leaders come out of the womb as leaders and simply wait until they are old enough to take their rightful place in society" (1995, 197). The reality is that leaders need to be developed. What are we as leaders doing to develop the leaders of tomorrow?

Peter and John became leaders because Jesus encouraged and equipped them. Do we focus on people's past or their potential? Are we investing in leadership development? If so, how are we developing those leaders? Geiger and Peck state,

> Leaders are developed as **knowledge** (truth), **experiences** (posture), and **coaching** (leaders) converge. All three are essential for a leader to be developed. Knowledge is what leaders must learn and know. Experiences encompass the ongoing opportunities to serve and put knowledge into practice. Coaching occurs when a shepherding leader applies the knowledge and experience with a new leader (2016, 163).

These three items are consistent with what we note about Jesus's training of the twelve. Our Lord put the right people on the bus and then educated them (knowledge), involved them (experiences), and evaluated/encouraged/empowered them (coaching). How does this look in our churches?

Are We Getting the Right People in the Right Seats?

We Need the Right People on the Bus

In *Equipping 101*, Maxwell states, "There is something much more important and scarce than ability: It is the ability to recognize ability" (2003, 37). I would add that there is an even greater need to recognize spirituality, or relationship with and embodiment of Jesus. We desperately need leaders. But the only thing worse than not having leaders is having ungodly leaders in the Lord's church. As brother J. W. McGarvey once said, "A very small wolf in sheep's clothing can scatter a large flock of sheep" (2010, 35). Do we make sure leaders are living godly lives and know God's word, or do we focus more on charisma and financial resources? Rushing to put people into key leadership positions can have dire consequences. Paul taught that elders are to be "able to teach" (1 Tim. 3:2; cf. Titus 1:9). James said that teachers "will be judged with greater strictness" (Jas. 3:1). With greater power comes greater accountability. Maybe that is why Paul said that deacons were first to be tested to see if they are blameless before appointing them to their roles (1 Tim. 3:10). My friend, Jerrie Barber, recommended, for example, that the wives and children of potential elders should be interviewed, and that these interviews should be conducted separately from the husband/father (Barber 2015, 95–96). Household management is a key characteristic for elders (1 Tim. 3:4–5). These interviews give insight into the character of both the potential elder and the family.

Now let me stress that no one is going to be perfect. I have seen congregations and individuals who try to hold potential elders and deacons to standards that are completely unreasonable. Paul says elders are to be above reproach (Titus 1:6–7), but that does not mean they will be perfect. Remember that only one perfect person has walked this planet. Having said this, I will stress that we need to make sure that we are appointing godly leaders and that they continue to be godly after appointment.

Paul also says that elders "must be well thought of by outsiders" (1 Tim. 3:7). Do we get input from respected people in the community when appointing leaders? Do we run background checks on elders, deacons, preachers, and Bible class teachers? I frequently encourage youth ministers to get background checks on all who work around their young people. The camps I work with now require it. We need to make sure we are getting the right people on the bus.

We Need to Make Sure We Get the Right People into the Right Seats

I mentioned earlier that one of my first priorities when I arrived at Heritage Christian University was to make sure that we had the right people on the bus and in the right seats. There were a couple of experienced presidents who said I should basically start over with new employees if I wanted to be successful. These presidents, and others, also told me that I needed to clarify the vision of the university and make sure employees were committed to that vision.

It was the latter advice, not the former, that I chose to follow. To use a maritime analogy, I needed to know which employees were sails for our ship, and which employees were anchors holding us back. I found that we had an amazing group of individuals working for the school who were selflessly committed to our mission. They were sails, not anchors. However, I felt that some of the sails would be more effective if they were in a different part of the ship. To shift back to our bus analogy, they were the right people to have on the bus, but maybe some were not in the best seats for their skillsets. When we got them in the right positions, they blossomed, and the university was blessed.

I remember having one of those plastic Tupperware shape sorter balls when my siblings and I were kids. One half of the ball was red, and the other half was blue. It was hollow inside with several yellow pieces in different shapes: a star, a circle, a square, etc. Each half of the ball had a yellow handle that you could use to pull it apart for the shapes to fall out. There were openings cut in the sides of the ball that were consistent with the shaped pieces: a star, a circle, a square, etc. We spent hours pouring out the shapes, pushing them through the appropriate opening, and opening the ball to pour the shapes out and do it all over again. It is where we learned that you do not put a square shape in a round hole.

For some reason, we have struggled to figure this out in church work. We sometimes choose areas of ministry because we heard some other congregation was doing it and we thought it would be a good thing to do. We may not consider whether it is actually needed in our area. Just because a ministry is trendy does not mean it is best for all communities. Sometimes we do ministries simply because we always have, without considering whether they are still needed or effective. Sometimes, when assigning deacons or Bible class teachers, we place someone in an area of ministry based simply on their availability and/or the fact we have a position open and just need someone to fill it, whether or not they are actually a good fit. Before I proceed, let me stress that people can and should be stretched. People can learn new things. Leaders can develop new passions. We regularly see leaders in Scripture doing this (cf. Moses). Yet, I would like to suggest that instead of just plugging deacons into a ministry because we need someone in a spot, maybe ministries and deacons would be more successful if we considered the experiences, capabilities, and passions of those who might lead them. Maybe we should work on putting round shapes in round holes.

Areas of ministry in local congregations should grow out of need, opportunity, and capability. It is not uncommon to hear someone talk about the need to be culturally aware. I would like to add that leaders need to be communally and congregationally aware. If we know culture, community, and congregation, then we can design ministries that meet needs, take advantage of opportunities, and utilize the capabilities, experiences, and passions of the members.

I have worked at some amazing places and with some wonderful people. I have also, at times, chosen to leave some of those places because the vision leadership had for my work prevented me from doing the things that I was most passionate about. In any area of work, you will do things you are not as passionate about, but you do it because you were asked to do it by your leaders, or you know it is important or needed. Workers will not necessarily be excited about everything they are asked to do. Most workers accept that. What will cut short their tenure is not getting to do anything they are passionate about or not getting to do what they are most passionate about. Churches would be wise to not only consider community and congregational needs when developing ministries and appointing ministry leaders, but also to consider the passions and capabilities of potential leaders. Put round shapes in round holes. Make sure that everyone on the bus is in the right seat.

Are We Preparing the Passengers?

Leadership preparation needs to be part of the DNA of every congregation of the Lord's church. My disserta-

tion was titled "A Cross-Cultural Study of Factors Motivating Church of Christ Ministry Students to Enter
Ministry." I looked at Bible majors from twenty brotherhood schools in four countries: the U.S., Panama, India,
and Nigeria. I wanted to know what the factors were that
motivated them to want to be leaders/teachers in the
Lord's church. Participants were given twenty-nine potential factors to choose from. Students could list more than
one influence. Here are the top fifteen influences for
students in the United States:

1. A desire to help people (85.2 percent).
2. A feeling that God gave them gifts/abilities that
   they should use (77.6 percent).
3. A concern for those who are spiritually lost (71.4
   percent).
4. God had used events in their lives to lead them
   toward ministry (65.5 percent).
5. Previous experience in ministry (internships,
   etc.) (57.9 percent).
6. Family influence (49.5 percent).
7. Youth minister influence (42.4 percent).
8. Preacher influence (39.9 percent).
9. Teaching in the congregation (39.5 percent).
10. Training outside their congregation (camps, etc.)
    (38.8 percent).
11. A desire to counter false teaching (38.2 percent).
12. A leader outside their congregation (38.2
    percent).
13. A sermon they heard (38.2 percent).
14. Something they read in Scripture (34.9 percent).
15. An adult in the congregation (not an elder,

deacon, preacher, youth minister, or teacher)
(34.5 percent).

Several observations might be made from this. First of all, these students decided to train for ministry because of internal motivations. This is clear in the top four factors in our list. They were motivated by concern for others and the sense that God had given them abilities and opportunities to be leaders for God. Factors 1–4 likely grew out of factors 5 and following. Let us combine what the study revealed with Jesus's practice of educating His apostles.

Education

How do we instill the four top factors above in Bible students so that they will be motivated to be spiritual leaders? My research identified three key areas where this education takes place: the home, the congregation, and the camp.

In the Home

My research revealed that the most important people influencing Bible majors were family members, especially parents. In their landmark study of faith retention in adolescents that is described in the book *Soul Searching*, Christian Smith and his team made the following primary conclusion:

> Contrary to popular misguided cultural stereotypes and frequent parental misperceptions, we believe that the evidence clearly shows that the single most important

social influence on the religious and spiritual lives of adolescents is their parents (Smith 2005, 261).

My research revealed that almost half of the Bible majors in the study said they were training for ministry in the church because of their families. Families influenced them more than anyone else. Leadership development starts in the home. I often tell parents that if they are concerned that there are not enough leaders and preachers in the church, then they should do something about it. They are the ones with the most power and influence. What they talk about and value is what their children will talk about and value. What they put into practice is what their children will put into practice. For example, Wesley Black researched the reasons teenagers drop out of church after leaving the youth group and reported his findings in an article titled "Stopping the Dropouts" in the *Christian Education Journal*. He observes, "Teenagers whose fathers were involved in three or more volunteer leadership roles tended to go to church more during their young adult years" (Black 2008, 34).

In the Congregation

My dissertation also revealed the influence of what students read in Scripture or heard in sermons and Bible classes. What we preach and teach from God's word matters. What they hear about the roles of elders and deacons, for example, should not only come from a few lessons delivered a week or two before the congregation appoints new leaders. Teaching godly leadership and spiritual leadership roles should be built into sermons and Bible class lessons that they hear from birth up. Preachers and education directors need to develop plans to make sure this happens. We cannot start too young.

We need to go beyond leadership in worship. My parents were among five families who helped to start a congregation in Lebanon Junction, Kentucky. Because we had so many new Christians, the men started a men's/boys' class focused on leading in worship. I think of brother Earl Moore. He was so soft-spoken that you could barely hear him say his name. It was amazing to see the transformation in him that took place after the class, as he started participating in public worship. Such classes have blessed many congregations and leaders over the years. There are many organized programs now to train young people for leadership and ministry. Unfortunately, many of these programs have reduced leadership to leading in worship or in a Bible class. These are areas in which spiritual leaders lead, but spiritual leadership involves so much more. We do not need leaders who just know how to lead singing; we need leaders who know how to lead godly congregations, how to lead people to Christ, and how to lead in godly ways in any area of leadership in which they find themselves.

We need to remember that ladies need to be trained as spiritual leaders as well. Don't misunderstand me; I am not saying that we should violate Scripture and start appointing women as elders, deacons, and preachers. What I am saying is that there are many arenas in which women can practice leadership that are consistent with God's word. Ladies' days and ladies' devotionals are common in most congregations. This requires ladies to lead singing, read Scripture, or teach God's word in front of other ladies. They deserve training in these areas as well. As I have noted, leadership is not just about leading in worship. There are other settings in which women lead in and out of the church. When they do so, they need to know how to be godly leaders. Who is going to invest time in training and encouraging them?

Current leaders need to remember the importance of their influence and example. People rarely rise above the example of their leaders. Leaders need to make sure they are leading in godly ways if they want to develop godly leaders in the congregation. They need to set an example of growing as leaders as well. They should be known for reading books, watching videos, and attending conferences and workshops to be better leaders. This will inspire those who are around them to do the same. They should be identifying future leaders that they can encourage. I suggest that all congregations develop an organized leadership training program. In addition to being systemic in regular Bible classes and sermons, this could include special Bible classes for future elders and deacons, a leadership resource section of the church library (books, videos, audios), attending conferences and workshops, bringing in guest speakers to conduct seminars, mentoring by older leaders, and panel discussions featuring experienced leaders.

In the Camp

My dissertation survey also identified the role of leadership training outside the congregation (cf. factors 10 and 12). My parents started sending me to preacher and leadership training camps when I was in high school. These had a profound impact on my life. It was at the Future Preachers Training Camp at the Pennington Bend church of Christ in Nashville, Tennessee in July 1982 that I made the decision to preach God's word. I later worked on the staff of that camp as well as the Middle Tennessee Future Ministers Camp, Horizons Leadership Camp at FHU, and TITUS Camp at HCU. Since 2010, I have been working under the oversight of the Forrest Park church of Christ in Valdosta, GA, to start future minister camps throughout Latin America. As of the writing of this book, God has worked through Chuck Morris, me, and several of our friends to start camps in ten Latin American countries. We are currently planning to add our eleventh country. I have seen firsthand the difference these kinds of camps, that bring young people and experienced leaders together, can make in preparing future leaders. Churches are able to do collectively what is more difficult for some of them to do individually.

Conclusion

An Associated Press article notes, "Eight times since 1995, the American men have either been disqualified or failed to get the baton around the track at the Olympics or world championships" (Pells 2016). Relay teams and corporations must learn to pass the leadership baton, and so must God's people. While teaching at Freed-Hardeman University, I would give all of our youth ministry graduates a baton. It had the school's logo, the date of their graduation, 2 Timothy 2:2, and "It's Your Turn" etched on the side. I wanted to remind them of what had been given to them and likewise their responsibility to pass it on to someone else. To whom are you going to pass the baton?

Discussion Questions

1. What did you find most helpful in this lesson?
2. Make a list of things that your congregation could do to better train current and future leaders.
3. Why do you think we struggle with evaluation in the church?
4. What are some things we can do to better show our appreciation for current leaders and to give encouragement to future leaders?

Homework

1. Elders—Work together to make a list of individuals in the congregation whom you think could be future elders or deacons. Develop a plan for training and mentoring those individuals.
2. Deacons—Identify someone younger than you whom you are going to mentor personally to be a deacon.
3. All participants—Make a list of people whom you think would be excellent leadership mentors. Ask one or two of them if they will mentor you.

11

COACH (PART 2)
HE TRAINED THE NEXT GENERATION

Introduction

PROLIFIC LEADERSHIP AUTHOR and University of Michigan Business School professor Noel Tichy made the following statement in the foreword to his book *The Cycle of Leadership*: "Perhaps the No. 1 responsibility of a CEO is to develop other leaders who can carry on the legacy of the organization" (2002, xxiii). Each corporation, country, and church is potentially one generation from its demise. If leadership in one generation does not prepare the next generation of leaders, then they destroy the bridge that carries their accomplishments and impact into the future. Let us continue our focus on what Jesus did to develop the apostles and how these actions might help us.

The Christ

MacArthur states the following in his book *Twelve Ordinary Men*: "Christ personally chose the Twelve and invested most of His energies in them" (2002, 3). He goes on to add, "The process of choosing and calling them happened in distinct stages" (MacArthur 2002, 3). He notes that they were called to conversion, to ministry, to apostleship, and then to martyrdom (MacArthur 2002, 3–5). We began talking about the stages of development/commitment for followers of Christ in the last chapter. We also started considering what Jesus did to develop the apostles: getting the right people on the bus and educating them in godliness and leadership. We continue our analysis of Jesus's leadership training techniques by noting additional ways He prepared them for ministry: He involved them, evaluated and encouraged them, and handed over the keys.

Jesus Prepared Them for Ministry

In our last lesson we emphasized that once Jesus put the right men on the "apostolic bus," He began their preparation with education. In other words, He taught them how to live godly lives and how to practice godly leadership. Now let us look at the next stages in the preparation process: involvement, evaluation, and encouragement.

He Involved Them in Ministry

He gave them hands-on opportunities to practice what He taught them. I think of Paul's guidance concerning deacons: "Let them also be tested first" (1 Tim. 3:10). An example of this can be found in Luke 9:1–5. (He did something similar with seventy disciples in Luke 10.) It is worth noting that He gave them very specific instructions for what they were to do and not do (Luke 9:3–5; Matt. 10:5–11:1).

The instructions in Matthew 10 are much more detailed than those in Luke 9. As we look at these detailed instructions, there are two key things that are worth noticing. First of all, Jesus gave them a job description, including not only what they should do but also what they were not to do (10:5–8). Secondly, He gave protocols for how to do their jobs and even how to handle problems (10:9–25). In the process, Jesus taught us the importance of preparing workers and giving clarity on jobs and protocols.

He Evaluated Them

Jesus sent them out on small "mission trips" where they put their learning into practice, and then He debriefed them upon their return. "On their return the apostles told him all that they had done" (Luke 9:10). We see the same thing happening when the seventy returned in Luke 10:17. They bragged, "Lord, even the demons are subject to us in your name!" (10:17). Jesus corrected them by saying,

> I saw Satan fall like lightning from heaven. Behold, I have given you authority to tread on serpents and scorpions, and over all the power of the enemy, and nothing shall hurt you. Nevertheless, do not rejoice in this, that the spirits are subject to you, but rejoice that your names are written in heaven (Luke 10:18–20).

The twelve and the seventy reported the work they had done, and Jesus evaluated them. There is a saying in leadership circles, "You cannot manage what you do not measure." Evaluation is important.

He Also Encouraged Them

He encouraged them before they became apostles. An example of this is in John 1. Andrew was a follower of John the immerser, who had prepared his followers to become followers of the Messiah. When Andrew learned that Jesus of Nazareth was that Messiah, he went and told his brother, Simon. When Simon was brought to Jesus, the Savior said, "'You are Simon the son of John? You shall be called Cephas' (which means Peter)" (John 1:42). "Peter" means "rock" or "stone." Can you imagine being given a nickname by the Son of God? One of my daughters' favorite actors is former wrestler and football player DeWayne Johnson. His nickname is "the Rock." He is known for his strength. Even before Simon became an apostle, Jesus saw strength in him. In light of this, He changed his name to "the Rock." He called him a rock every time He called his name (in the back of my mind I hear the crowd chanting, "Rocky, Rocky, Rocky," in the old Rocky movies). Jesus built a rock out of Simon. He called him a rock until he became one. People will often live up to, or down to, what we call them.

We also see Jesus's encouragement in Matthew 10. We have already noted the detailed instructions that Jesus gave here. He clarified their jobs and the protocols that would guide their actions. Those protocols included how to deal with rejection and persecution. He warned them that persecution was coming but then motivated them to fulfill their tasks anyway (10:26–42). Four times in this section He tells them either not to be anxious or not to fear (10:19, 26, 28, 31). Jesus corrected the twelve when necessary but encouraged them constantly. That is likely one reason they were willing to die for Him.

Jesus Handed Over the Keys

We continue our "bus" analogy by noting that Jesus turned over the keys to the apostles. He literally told Peter, "I will give you the keys of the kingdom of heaven" (Matt. 16:19). This was fulfilled when Peter preached that powerful sermon that led to the conversion of 3,000 souls in Acts 2. Jesus gave them real power and real authority. He gave them authority over demons and disease (Matt. 10:1). Twice He told them, "Whatever you bind on earth shall be bound in heaven" (Matt. 16:19; 18:18). When Jesus sent the apostles out in pairs (Luke 10:1), He trusted that they would do the right thing. After His death, Jesus did not send angels to tell the world of His death and the way of salvation. He sent "earthen vessels" to share the good news (cf. 2 Cor. 4:7–10; Acts 1:8). There were times in the ministry of the apostle Paul in which Jesus and the Spirit interceded to guide Paul and his companions with very specific directions (cf. Acts 16:6–7). Yet often Jesus seems to have allowed Paul to make his own decisions concerning where he would go next to spread the kingdom. The point is that Jesus trusted the fate of the world to these men. He chose the right men and then trusted them to make the right decisions.

The Christian

Peter seems to have had some innate ability to lead, but it needed a lot of work. He needed someone who would believe in him and invest in him as a leader. Maxwell observes,

When was the last time you went out of your way to make people feel special, as if they were somebody? The investment required on your part is totally overshadowed by the impact it makes on them. Everyone you know and all the people you meet have the potential to be someone important in the lives of others. All they need is encouragement and motivation from you to help them reach their potential (*Relationships* 2003, 17).

Inclusion

Geiger and Peck note, "Church leaders must confidently invite people to serve, knowing that the opportunities to serve provide moments where development occurs" (2016, 174). They go on to add, "Ministry experiences present many teachable moments, and when those moments are shepherded by a godly leader, development increases" (Geiger and Peck 2016, 175). Did you notice in the last chapter that "previous experience" was number 5 on my list of factors influencing the decision to train for church ministry? Almost 58 percent of the students in my study said they were preparing to be leaders because they had the opportunity to experience leadership as a young person before making their decision. In the "Stopping the Dropouts" article I referred to in the last chapter, Black observes, "Those who led church programs are more likely to attend church as young adults" (2008, 35).

Many churches have summer internship programs for college students, especially in youth ministry. Let me add that I wish more churches would do internships in other areas of ministry, especially preaching. I appreciated my friend and former coworker, Matt Winkler, for something he did at a congregation we worked at together. He conducted a summer internship for several of the young men within the congregation (most churches use interns from other congregations). Many of those young men are leaders today because of those experiences.

Another way you can develop leaders is by seeking their input. For example, the next time you are seeking to hire a youth minister or preacher, include some teens and twenty-somethings on your search committee. Not only will you gain valuable input, but the inclusion of these voices will develop them as leaders. I encourage "ride-along" programs. Law enforcement uses this approach all the time. I ran into one of my former students while visiting his congregation and learned that he was a policeman. I asked him how he ended up in that line of work. He said he did a ride-along with a police officer, and they became involved in a high-speed chase. He was hooked. I have frequently taken teenagers with me when I conduct Bible studies. We have divided campers at our ministry training camps up and assigned them to experienced leaders. Those leaders would then take the campers visiting at the hospital or door knocking in the community. Why not invite deacons to sit in on elders' meetings periodically or to go visiting with older elders? I find it shocking that new elders often sit in on an elders' meeting for the first time when they are appointed as an elder or when they are being interviewed for potential appointment as an elder. One of the best ways to train leaders is by joining experienced leaders as they lead.

Evaluation

What Will You Evaluate?

A general rule of thumb in leadership is that you cannot evaluate what you do not articulate. Leadership preparation should include clear guidance (articulation) for those chosen to lead areas of ministry. One of the biggest mistakes that organizations and churches make is that they do not provide job descriptions for key roles. In her book *Volunteer Orientation and Training*, Wilson notes, "If you expect volunteers to uphold standards, you've got to make clear what those standards are" (2004 *Orientation*, 31). Here are six reasons job descriptions are important.

1. It is impossible to hit a target that has never been set up. You need to know what leaders want you to aim at. This will also help workers to prioritize their actions. The problem is that many leaders do not know what they want from employees or volunteers.
2. If there is not one, there will be many. In the vacuum of no written job description, you will find that deacons and preachers operate under many job descriptions. Each elder has one in his head, and most of the members have one as well. No one can live up to all these demands.
3. In the absence of something, you will be expected to do everything. Job descriptions provide barriers for workers and volunteers to keep them from having more and more dumped

on them. Workers need some kind of protection from being asked to do too much.

4. When we do not know who is supposed to do it, either everybody fights over doing it, or nobody does it. Neither is healthy for making progress or for building unity and teamwork.

5. You will be held accountable for things you were never told were important. An Olympic gymnast knows exactly what the judges are looking for before walking out on the mat. Can you imagine what it would be like to play a football game if none of the players knows the rules the referees were looking for or how the scorekeeper was going to keep score? Unfortunately, that is how we sometimes do leadership in the church.

6. People forget, and elders come and go. This is not an issue of integrity; it is an issue of memory. Elders are bombarded with information. Sometimes they just forget certain details. We all do. This is one reason I always tried to give a written summary of anything I was proposing to or sharing with the elders of the churches that I worked with. Also, there will be changes in the eldership. Having minutes of all meetings and written job descriptions helps leaders to conduct themselves with integrity toward workers and to honor agreements made with them in the past (even if the members of the eldership change).

Job descriptions should include (1) a clear description of

job responsibilities, (2) identification of areas of authority to make decisions (including what rights the worker has to spend money), (3) clarity on the chain of command (who they answer to), (4) parameters on the length of the job and how both sides can terminate it, (5) protocols and ethical principles that guide worker/leader actions, and (6) a "who to call" list for when the worker has needs or something goes wrong. Without job descriptions work is often left undone.

How Will You Evaluate?

Job descriptions and evaluation go hand in hand. Remember, you cannot evaluate what you do not articulate. Once job descriptions have been articulated, then you have paved the way for regular evaluation. In his landmark book, *The Five Dysfunctions of a Team*, Patrick Lencioni identifies dysfunction #4 as "avoidance of accountability" (2002, 189). Everyone at Heritage Christian University is evaluated. Even our board is evaluated. When I evaluate our vice presidents and my executive assistant, the first section of the evaluation has their current job description. The first two questions after the job description are (1) "Is there anything you are doing that is not listed on the job description?" and (2) "Is there anything that you are doing that should be elsewhere?" We are both being evaluated. I am being evaluated based on whether I gave them clear guidance on their responsibilities and on whether I provided the resources they need. They are evaluated based on how they carry out those responsibilities. When I worked at Freed-Hardeman University, I was evaluated by my immediate supervisor every year and by my students in every class.

Unfortunately, evaluation rarely happens in congregations (except for the elders occasionally evaluating preachers/youth ministers). I would recommend that there be some kind of annual or at least bi-annual evaluation of deacons, preachers, office staff, and Bible class teachers. There are many ways this might happen, but it should happen. You could have someone observe them, you could have an annual interview, you could have them fill out a report on what they did during the year, you could ask for Bible class teachers' lesson plans, or you could talk to students in their classes. You could give church leaders a form on which they list things they did to improve in their area of work in the past year, one thing they did that worked well, one area they need to improve on, and what they plan to do in the next year to grow as a leader.

I gave out a periodic "sermon survey" to the churches I worked with. I might ask questions like, "What question would you like to have addressed in a sermon or class?" "What book in the Bible have you studied the least?" or "What is your favorite verse?" I would also include questions like, "What is one thing that I do in preaching that you like?" or "What is one thing I do in preaching that you wish I would do differently?" No eldership ever asked me to do this. Most of them thought I was crazy for inviting people to criticize me. I did it because it made me a better preacher. Our vice presidents at HCU know that I am evaluated by the Board. There is also a survey sent to all employees every other year that allows them to evaluate me. I have shared with my leadership team things the Board wants me to work on. Transparency is important in leadership. I told them it is not fair for me to identify things they need to work on and for them not to know things I have been asked to work on. No one should be above being evaluated.

This includes elderships. Do congregations have any mechanism in place to verify that elders (and deacons) remain qualified? Just because they were qualified when appointed does not mean they remain so. Being an elder is not an honorary title you wear for life. It is a descriptive term for a godly man who serves in a body of godly leaders who have been appointed by the congregation (and sealed by the Spirit, Acts 20:28; Eph. 4:30) to guide God's people in that congregation toward God's goals for God's glory. When he no longer lives a godly life (habitual unrepentant sin) or is no longer able to lead God's people toward God's goals for God's glory (due to age, long-term illness, etc.), then he should no longer be considered an elder of the congregation. If an elder falls into one of these categories, he should step down. He should not force the congregation to take action.

It is important to remember that no one is perfect. This includes elders. We must also remember that the criteria for evaluation is God's word: 1 Timothy 3, Titus 1, and 1 Peter 5 in particular. Just because a group of elders made a decision that members disagreed with is not grounds for removing them (unless the decision violates God's word). Also, some leaders are stronger leaders than others. Being a weak leader is not the same as being an ungodly leader (though a weak leader should work to improve). The characteristics given by Paul focus on integrity and godly conduct. The point remains that just because someone was qualified when appointed, it does not mean that he remains qualified.

In light of this, there must be some means for members

to evaluate the continuing biblical soundness and godliness of their existing elders while still honoring them as leaders. The two best passages to guide us in dealing with wayward elders are Matthew 18:15–20 and 1 Timothy 5:1–2, 17–22. Some key principles gleaned from these passages, especially 1 Timothy 5, would be 1) respect for and appreciation of elders, 2) there must be evidence and multiple witnesses, 3) there should not be a rush to judgment (cf. "Do not lay hands upon anyone too quickly and thereby share responsibility for the sins of others," NASB), 4) the process should be led by the spiritually mature (Paul was talking to his coworker, Timothy), and 5) the elders are to be given an opportunity to repent and change (cf. "persist in sin," 1 Tim. 5:20).

I have heard of congregations that have periodic reaffirmations of the elders. There are benefits and dangers to this. A benefit, in my opinion, is that it creates a regular, orderly, and less confrontational way to determine if members are still comfortable with the biblical qualities of their leaders. There are also dangers involved. My friend J. J. Turner reminds us to exercise caution here (Turner 2005, 101). We would do well to heed his warning. However, I do not agree with his assessment that reaffirming elders is unbiblical. I am prepared to say that some methods of reaffirming are unbiblical, but not that the concept itself is.

We know that elders are to be appointed. We know that they must meet the characteristics God gives us in 1 Timothy 3 and Titus 1. We also know that they must continue to embody these qualities if they are to continue to serve as elders (cf. 1 Tim. 5). All of these things require some kind of congregational involvement and evaluation. Scripture does not give us a great deal of specific detail about how this is to be done. For example, there is no exact biblical example for announcing the names of potential elders and asking the church to contact certain individuals or to put their concerns in writing over the next two weeks if they see a reason any of them should not serve as an elder. I believe this is biblical because it is consistent with principles we see in Scripture (Acts 6; 14:23; 1 Timothy 3; Titus 1). Likewise, I recognize that we do not have an exact biblical example for reaffirming the elders every five years. But we do know from the Bible that elders must remain qualified, so there must be some kind of means of assessing this.

However, brother Turner is absolutely right in warning us of the dangers of reaffirmation. This should not be some kind of congregational show of hands in which weak members get to vote someone out. There is a real danger of division here. There is also a danger that elders or preachers who want power or to get even with someone might use such a process in a very un-Christlike way (cf. Turner 2005, 101). I have not worshipped with a congregation that practiced reaffirmation, and I have not suggested it to any congregation. I discuss it here, not out of a desire to promote it, but out of a desire to challenge those who practice it to consider their motivations and whether the process they use is consistent with Scripture. Here are some principles that I glean from personal reflections and principles I see in Matthew, Acts, 1 Timothy, and Titus.

1. It would seem wise to use a system similar to the process by which we appoint elders in the first place. Their names are put forward (possibly with new elders that are being proposed) and

members are given a period of time to respond. I do not recommend having some kind of vote (this gives the spiritually immature too much power).

2. The process should be led by the spiritually mature and care should be observed to make sure there is no conflict of interest involved for those leading the process.

3. Evidence should be required. No empty accusations should be accepted. Elders should be protected from unfounded and hidden attacks. Generally speaking, people should be required to sign their names to accusations, and they should go talk to the person in person first (cf. Matt. 18:15). Yet, we need to have caution in this area if potential abuse has taken place. It could be dangerous for someone who has been abused to face their abuser. Congregations need to provide opportunities for both the accused and the abused to be fairly and safely heard. Heritage Christian University professors Dr. Bill Bagents and Dr. Rosemary Snodgrass have written a book called *Counseling for Church Leaders* that I would recommend that you read.

4. The elders or potential elders should be respected and treated like family. Love should permeate this whole process.

5. The goal should be to honor God and do what is best for His church and to do what brings glory to His name.

Elders can build rapport in the congregation and show

their integrity by leading in the designing of a system whereby members can give input on their soundness.

Encouragement

Jesus not only evaluated the apostles; He also encouraged them. Before addressing the need for leaders to encourage those they train, I want to stress that followers need to encourage the leaders they follow. God has allowed me to work underneath amazing elderships over the years. They were selfless, sacrificial, and godly men. Preachers often see elders doing things and making sacrifices that no one else sees. I regularly encourage preachers and youth ministers to brag on their elders every chance they get. Make sure the congregation knows that you genuinely love and respect them. The members will often follow your lead. Frequently, elders only hear from members when they complain.

The focus of this chapter is on coaching or training the next generations of leaders. Thus, I want to encourage experienced leaders to encourage those coming behind them. I am a preacher today because people like Joe and Dorothy Brothers, Benny Burns, Pete Johnson, Tom Holland, Marlin Connelly, William Woodson, Rodney Cloud, Mike Brumley, Billy Smith, and so many more encouraged me to be a leader for the Lord. I spent a great deal of time in this chapter talking about the need for evaluation in the church. I did so because it is something that we either do not do or do not do well. I do not want to leave the impression that leaders should be looking for the faults in others. That is far from the truth. In fact, I have found that times of evaluation often include much more encouragement than correction. Evaluation is not about nitpicking and faultfinding. It is analyzing what is being done by others so that a leader may praise what is good and help others to correct what needs improvement. Encouragement and praise should flow out of every period of evaluation.

Likewise, encouragement should be part of the everyday process of building future leaders. Life is hard. People need encouragement. My executive assistant and I send well over 400 cards per year to people. When on campus at HCU, I will frequently walk the halls to stick my head in people's offices to see how they are doing, to brag on their work, and to thank them. In my work with young people, I have seen many a young man who was heartbroken because his first sermon did not go like he wanted it to. There will come a time when he will need guidance on how to improve the sermon, but what he most needs immediately afterward is the encouragement to keep on trying.

Leadership training and encouragement are everyone's business, not just those in the "big" leadership positions. Did you notice that over one-third of those who participated in my study (see p. 139–141) said they wanted to train for leadership ministry in the church because of an adult in their congre-gation? Elders, deacons, teachers, preachers, and youth ministers were all other choices on the survey. Thus, they were saying that they were influenced by adults who did not hold any of these positions. Heaven only knows how many have become preachers over the years because a sweet widow lady encouraged them to preach after hearing their first feeble attempt at a Wednesday night devotional. Jesus encouraged the disciples, and we should do the same.

Have We Turned over the Keys?

Kara Powell, Jake Mulder, and Brad Griffin talk about the concept of "key-chain leadership" in their book, *Growing Young*. The authors conducted research to determine what congregations can do in order to keep young people, ages 15 to 29, at the congregation. They identified ten falsehoods about growth that most people believe to be true. They also found six key principles that are fundamental for churches to "grow young." The first principle they highlight in the book is "Unlock Keychain Leadership: Sharing Power with the Right People at the Right Time" (Powell, Mulder, and Griffin 2016, 50). It is built on the concept that keys symbolize power.

> Whoever holds the keys has the power to let people in or keep people out. Keys provide access to physical rooms, as well as to strategic meetings, significant decisions, and central roles or places of authority. The more power you have, the more keys you tend to process (Powell, Mulder, and Griffin 2016, 53).

The authors go on to state that keychain leaders are "intentional about entrusting and empowering all generations, including teenagers and emerging adults, with their own set of keys" (Powell, Mulder, and Griffin 2016, 53). When we give our children the keys to the car, we are showing them that we trust them, and this is a vital step in the process of their maturity.

I remember well the day my youngest daughter was given the keys to the front door of the business where she got her first job out of college. That was a statement of trust from her employer. Jesus gave the apostles real trust and authority. He seems to have done it in phases, consistent with their level of maturity, but He gave them authority. Sometimes church leaders are reluctant to share the keys of power. I see this regularly in the mission field. I believe that one reason we do not have more elders in certain countries is that preachers are reluctant to give up power (though this is by no means the only reason).

We have this problem in the U.S. as well. Mentoring people takes time. You will actually lose time for a while if you let others play significant roles. However, if we will be patient, in the end more work will be done, and more people will be able to use their gifts for God's glory. One area, in particular, where I see reluctance to release the leadership keys is in the work of deacons. If deacons cannot spend money to accomplish their work, they have no power. If deacons cannot spend money, then elders do not trust them, and they know it.

We often point to Acts 6:1–7 as an example of the role of deacons. I am not prepared to say these are the first deacons, but I do think they can serve as decent prototypes. Seven men were put in charge of feeding the Greek-speaking widows, so the apostles could focus on preaching the word of God and prayer. Think of the types of things these men might have been responsible for in fulfilling their mission: gathering information, building relationships, gathering resources, mobilizing and training workers, organizing the process, evaluating successes/failures, giving reports to the apostles or the church, and handling the money needed to carry out their task. Think of how the appointment process worked. The apostles

- Recognized the need.
- Clarified job descriptions.
- Highlighted qualifications.
- Designed a collaborative process for congregational input.
- Installed them and stepped aside to let them do their work.

Brother James D. Cox, in his book *With the Bishops and Deacons*, has a powerful statement concerning deacons in general, and Acts 6 in particular:

> The very fact that they are "servants" disposed to be in readiness for *whatever* they may be asked to do may give a reason for no more specific biblical mention being made of their tasks. However, as in the case of the neglected Grecian widows in Acts 6, it is very reasonable to assume that the apostles let them do their job. The men were "appointed over this business" and it was, in all probability, organized by them as to all the details free and clear of the apostles. In the absence of further complications the apostles would have no further time or effort with the situation (1976, 23–24).

An often-repeated saying in church leadership circles is some version of the following: "The preacher is doing the work of the elders, the elders are doing the work of the deacons, and the deacons have no idea what they are doing or are supposed to do." This would not be true if elderships would practice the five steps listed above when appointing deacons. Elders need to stop doing the work of the deacons. People are dying without knowing Jesus, marriages are falling apart on a regular basis, and the sick and heart-broken are longing for someone to hold their hands and give them hope. Elders should not have time to sit in board-rooms and discuss the color of the paint or carpet. It is time to give up the keys. It is good to have budgets and account-ability for work and funds spent. Still, many a church is stymied in its work and growth because deacons and ministry leaders cannot make independent decisions and/or they are required to call an elder every time they spend any money in their areas of work. Let me say it again. If deacons cannot spend money, then you do not trust them, and they know it! If you don't trust them, then do not appoint them as deacons! If you appointed them as deacons, then trust them to spend money and report what they spent. If elders do not give up the "leadership keys," they should not be surprised if their congregations are still struggling when they are gone. Is that the legacy we want to leave behind?

Conclusion

Larry Bossidy, the former CEO of the Honeywell, stated,

> You won't remember when you retire what you did in the first quarter ... or the third. What you'll remember is how many people you developed, how many people you helped have a better career because of your interest and your dedication to their development (qtd. in Tichy 2002, xxvii).

Leadership guru Max De Pree stresses that leaders should leave behind assets and a legacy. In the business world, this can be financial health, products, services, tools, land, and facilities. He then adds, "But what else do leaders *owe*? What are artful leaders responsible for? Surely we need to include people. People are the heart and spirit of all that counts" (De Pree 2004, 13). Church leaders should leave a legacy of people who can lead. Moses trained Joshua, David trained Solomon, Jesus trained the twelve, Barnabas trained Paul, and Paul trained Timothy. Paul told Timothy, "You then, my child, be strengthened by the grace that is in Christ Jesus, and what you have heard from me in the presence of many witnesses entrust to faithful men, who will be able to teach others also" (2 Tim. 2:1–2). Who are the "faithful" ones to whom we are passing our heritage of leadership?

Discussion Questions

1. What did you find most helpful in this lesson?
2. What are some dangers of evaluation and what are some dangers of not evaluating?
3. Why do you think churches have so few job descriptions for key positions?

Homework

1. Make a list of all the positions in your congregation/company that do not have job descriptions.
2. If you are in a position of leadership, answer the following questions:

What have you done in the last year to improve as a leader?

What did you do as a leader this past year that you should keep doing?

What did you do as a leader this past year that you should change?

What are you going to do in the next year to improve as a leader?

12

CHARACTER

HE LIVED A LIFE OF INTEGRITY

Introduction

ONE OF THE most amazing things I have done is to become a beekeeper. Honeybees are fascinating. For example, one of the ways they communicate with each other is through dances. When a foraging bee finds a good location for pollen collection, she will return to the hive and do a waggle dance (forager bees are always females). She is basically recreating a "miniaturized reenactment of her recent flight outside the hive" (Seeley 2010, 10). The duration of her dance tells her sisters the distance to the site. In general, one second represents six-tenths of a mile. The angle of her dance tells other forgers the angle they should go out of the hive relative to the sun. For example, "If the waggling bee heads 40 degrees to the right of vertical, her message is, 'The feeding place is 40 degrees to the right of the sun'" (Seeley 2010, 11). I told you they were fascinating! Foraging bees are the oldest bees in the colony. Because of this, they have developed the best internal compasses, which allow them to find their way home and to communicate accurate messages to their sisters. Younger bees are more apt to get lost. It is not uncommon, for example, for young queens who are going out on their mating flights not to be able to find their way back to their hives. They have not developed their sense of direction, their internal compasses. The results can be deadly. What about our internal compasses?

We have mentioned researchers Kouzes and Posner several times in this book. They sum up their findings concerning leadership as follows:

> The most important personal quality people look for and admire in a leader is personal credibility. *Credibility is the foundation of leadership. If people don't believe in the messenger, they won't believe the message.* This finding has been so consistent for over twenty years that we've come to call it The First Law of Leadership (2004, 120).

William Cohen identifies the quality that research shows is most highly prized of those who lead in demanding and dangerous circumstances. "In simple terms, it's integrity: adherence to set of values that incorporate honesty and freedom from deception. But integrity is more than honesty. It means doing the right thing regardless of circumstances or inconvenience to the leader or the organization" (2010, 11). Webster's dictionary defines character as "moral excellence and firmness" (2002, 376) and integrity as "uncompromising adherence to a code of moral, artistic, or other values" (2002, 1174). Do we act in morally excellent ways? Do we have a moral code/compass, and is that code/compass from God? Abraham Lincoln said, "Character was like a tree, and reputation like its shadow. The shadow is what we think of it; the tree was the real thing" (Gross 1912, 109). Jesus Christ is known around the world 2,000 years after His death. Let us consider the majestic tree that casts such a long shadow.

The Christ

This lesson will focus on the character or integrity of Jesus Christ, the one who taught us how to live godly lives. We will begin by seeing that Jesus practiced what He preached. We will then emphasize this fact by looking at two difficult settings in which Jesus had the integrity to do the right thing. Come walk with us under the shade of Jesus's character.

Preaching

A key term in the preaching of Jesus is "hypocrite," *hupokritēs* in Greek. It is found seventeen times in the New Testament, and all of them are on the lips of Jesus. *Hupokritēs* means "actor, in the sense pretender" (Danker 2000, 1038) or "one who pretends to be other than he really is" (Louw and Nida 1989, 766). We noted earlier that Kouzes and Posner list credibility as the key leadership trait. They add, "And what is credibility behaviorally? We've asked this question thousands of times, and the most frequent response we get is, 'Do What You Say You Will Do,' or DWYSYWD for short" (2004, 120). It is the idea that we will do what we say we will do and that we are who we say we are. This is the opposite of a hypocrite. A hypocrite is someone who claims or pretends to be one thing, but they are in fact something else. This is summarized in Jesus's quote from Isaiah: "Well did Isaiah prophesy of you hypocrites, as it is written, 'This people honors me with their lips, but their heart is far from me'" (Mark 7:6; cf. Isaiah 29:13). Jesus repeatedly commanded His followers, "Do not be like the hypocrites" (Matt. 6:5; cf. 6:2, 16; 7:5). He pronounces "woe" on hypocrites seven times in Matthew 23. In Matthew 24 He says that hypocrites will be in the place where "there will be weeping and gnashing of teeth" (Matt. 24:51). The point is clear. Jesus did not want His people to be actors, fakes, or pretenders. He wanted them to be people of character, credibility, and integrity.

Practice

Peter's teaching in the home of Cornelius at Caesarea represented a critical moment in the spread of the gospel. I spent a month in the summer after the completion of my undergraduate degree digging in the sand of Caesarea as part of an archaeological team headed by Dr. Robert J. Bull of Drew University in New Jersey. During that period, I came to have great interest in and amazement for this magnificent city. Caesarea was the seat of Roman government in Judea. It represented the largest Gentile presence in an otherwise Jewish dominated region. It was in this city that God found a "God-fearing" Gentile. It was in this Roman centurion's home that Peter would proclaim that all human beings had been declared "clean" by God and could accept the salvation of the Lord. It is interesting to note how Peter introduced Jesus to Cornelius, his household, and his friends. Peter described Christ as one who "went about doing good" (Acts 10:38). Cornelius was a leader of men, a man of action. Peter proclaimed a man of action to a man of action. Jesus was a "doer." Jesus did not merely teach what was good; He went about doing what was good. That is what separates Him from many other would-be leaders.

In the book of Acts, the inspired writer Luke refers to his first book, the Gospel of Luke, as follows: "In the first book, O Theophilus, I have dealt with all that Jesus began to *do and teach*" (Acts 1:1, emphasis mine). Jesus did not merely talk the talk, but He also walked the walk. He practiced what He preached. That is why He was able to teach His apostles about service and say,

> You call me Teacher and Lord, and you are right, for so I am. If I then, your Lord and Teacher, have washed your feet, you also ought to wash one another's feet. For I have given you an example, that you also should do just as I have done to you (John 13:13–15).

Jesus referred to Himself as "the good shepherd" (cf. John 10:11, 14). This is an interesting analogy when it comes to teaching. Cattle are usually driven, but sheep are led. Jesus did not merely tell people how to walk, He walked through the valley ahead of them and showed them how to do it. Now let us consider the depth of Jesus's character as we see Him practice what He preached, even when it was painful or private.

Pain

Martin Luther King, Jr. stated, "The ultimate measure of a man is not where he stands in moments of comfort and convenience, but where he stands at times of challenge and controversy" (King 1984, 43). The writer of the book of Hebrews stated, "For we do not have a high priest who is unable to sympathize with our weaknesses, but one who in every respect has been tempted as we are, yet without sin" (Heb. 4:15). Let us focus on the most famous of those temptations, the challenges by Satan as recorded in Matthew 4 and Luke 4. Luke's account describes one of the temptations as follows:

> And the devil took him up and showed him all the kingdoms of the world in a moment of time, and said to him, 'To you I will give all this authority and their glory, for it has been delivered to me, and I give it to whom I will. If you, then, will worship me, it will all be yours' (Luke 4:5–7).

This temptation comes in the aftermath of Jesus's baptism and the beginning of His public ministry.

Temptations often present themselves when one makes a key decision for God. When I baptize people into Christ, I challenge them not to be surprised if Satan tries to discourage them or tempt them in the near future. If you read this book and make the decision to be a better leader, Satan will go after you. That is what he does. He is "a roaring lion, seeking someone to devour" (1 Pet. 5:8). Satan attacked Jesus in connection with His power and position. At His baptism, the Father declared, "You are my beloved Son" (Luke 3:22). Notice that two of the temptations began with "If you are the Son of God" (Luke 4:3, 9). Our areas of strength can also become targets for temptation. If you are good with money, then Satan will tempt you to gain it by immoral means, or he will tempt you to make it the most important thing in your life. If you have enough confidence to stand before a group of people and share God's word, Satan will tempt you to be prideful. If you have a talent for helping people in time of need, Satan will tempt you to step over the line in a counseling situation and into immorality.

Some question whether Satan could really give Jesus all the kingdoms of the earth (Luke 4:5–6). Satan is the father of lies (John 8:44), yet I believe he was telling the truth in this case. We know that God allows him to exercise certain freedoms in the world (cf. Job 1–2). We also know that he is referred to in the New Testament as "the god of this world" (2 Cor. 4:4) and "the ruler of this world" (John 12:31; 14:30; 16:11). John declared, "We know that we are from God, and the whole world lies in the power of the evil one" (1 John 5:19). Paul told the Philippian brethren concerning the exalted position of Jesus,

> Therefore God has highly exalted him and bestowed on him the name that is above every name, so that at the name of Jesus every knee should bow, in heaven and on earth and under the earth, and every tongue confess that Jesus Christ is Lord, to the glory of God the Father (Phil. 2:9–11).

But Paul also said that before Jesus enjoyed that exalta-tion He became "obedient to the point of death, even death on a cross" (Phil. 2:8).

The road to the crown was paved with a cross. Satan was offering Jesus a less painful way out. He offered Christ the option of deferring to Satan now or dying for sin later. Both would lead to a crown. One was easier than the other. How would Jesus respond? He replied with an emphatic, "Be gone, Satan! For it is written, 'You shall worship the

Lord your God and him only shall you serve'" (Matt. 4:10). This example is from the beginning of Christ's ministry, yet we see the same attitude at the end of His ministry. One hears it in those powerful words He spoke from the Garden of Gethsemane: "Not my will, but yours, be done" (Luke 22:42). Jesus was a man of character, no matter the pain or cost.

Privacy

One of the most famous quotes of John Wooden, former head basketball coach at UCLA, was, "The true test of a man's character is what he does when no one is watching" (quoted in Edmondson 2020, 57). The word "hypocrite" comes from Greek drama. It came to refer to those who claim or seem to be one thing but who are in fact something else (Kittel and Friedrich 1972, 562). When we step on the stage of life, we all tend to put on our masks and act like the person we want others to think we are. We hide the real us. It is only in private that we take the mask off and stop acting.

Let us return once again to the temptation of Jesus. Listen to Luke's introduction to the encounter between Christ and Satan: "And Jesus, full of the Holy Spirit, returned from the Jordan and was led by the Spirit in the wilderness for forty days, being tempted by the devil" (Luke 4:1–2). Did you notice that the temptation took place "in the wilderness"? Mark's account says He was "with the wild animals" (1:13). The audience for this real-life drama consisted of scorpions, snakes, and wild animals. The stage for this providential production consisted of desert sand and the rocky crags of a great mountaintop. In fact, Jesus stood on the pinnacle of the temple and refused the one temptation which would have flaunted His greatness before the people of Jerusalem. He would not cast Himself off that pinnacle just because He could. Jesus wasn't acting. He chose to have character instead of being a character.

How was Jesus able to do the right thing even when no one was looking? There are many possible answers, but there is one I would like to consider at this time. Mark's account says that after the temptations "the angels were ministering to him" (Mark 1:13). God sent heavenly encouragers. Jesus understood that, when the amphitheater of humanity was empty, there was another audience which was still watching. There is a heavenly balcony in the auditorium of life. Listen to what the Messiah says in the Sermon on the Mount: "But when you pray, go into your room and shut the door and pray to your Father who is in secret. And your Father who sees in secret will reward you" (Matt. 6:6). We never leave the Father's presence. People of character understand that there is an audience for every event of their lives. Remembering this is important to being a person of character and integrity.

The Christian

Now it is time to make this lesson personal. The book *The Extraordinary Leader* discusses the research findings of Zenger and Folkman. They identify five key traits of leaders and illustrate them by referring to them as tent poles in the "leadership tent." The outer poles are "Focus on Results," "Personal Capability," "Leading Organizational Change," and "Interpersonal Skills." Notice how similar these traits are to the habits of Jesus. The fifth trait they identified is

"Character." They describe it as the center pole of the tent. The reason for this is that, if a leader is not a person of character and integrity, the whole leadership tent comes down (2002, 53). This reminds me of one of my favorite quotes. It was a statement made by former U.S. Senator Alan K. Simpson while introducing former President Gerald R. Ford at Harvard in 1999. "If you have integrity, nothing else matters. If you don't have integrity, nothing else matters" (Simpson 1999).

Are we people of character? Elders of integrity honor agreements made with their preachers and youth ministers. Preachers of character honor promises made to congregations and practice what they preach. Youth ministers of integrity will never do anything inappropriate in their relationships with the young people in the congregation (or anyone else for that matter). Deacons with character will handle church funds in honest and upright ways. A person of character does what is right even if it costs a job or a promotion. A person of integrity does what is right even if no one is looking. A person of character will not look at pornographic movies or pictures late at night on the television or internet. Men of integrity are faithful to their wives even if no one will ever know.

I was asked to contribute a chapter for the book *Fit for the Pulpit*. I was assigned the chapter, "The Preacher and Sin." I found myself wondering why the editor, Chris McCurley, gave me that particular chapter! Here is what I observed while preparing the manuscript. Sin tends to come in three primary ways (1 John 2:15–16; Gen. 3; Luke 4:1–13):

1. Lust of the flesh—i.e., temptation to have

inappropriate relationships with members of the
opposite sex, or to love money and gain it
dishonestly.

2. Lust of the eyes—i.e., watching internet
pornography.

3. Pride of life—i.e., enjoying the praise of people
and sacrificing our principles and the truth to be
liked by people.

We overcome these temptations by watching and pray-ing.
Watching involves (1) acknowledging our areas of
weakness, (2) avoiding tempting situations, and (3) accessing
someone who will hold us accountable. Praying involves not
only confession and repentance but also seeking God's help
in fighting temptation.

Former professor Ian A. Fair observes, "Values form the
ethical glue that hold an organization together, the compass
that gives it direction, the integrity that gives it respectabil-
ity, and the parameters that give it stability" (2008, 77). The
older, more experienced forager bees in my hives are better
guides for the other honeybees in my colonies because they
have developed internal compasses. When those compasses
are off, the results can be lethal for the colony. That is even
more true spiritually. As leaders, we need to consider what
the internal values are that make up our internal
compasses, what are the sources of those values (God or
someone/something else), and whether or not we are living
lives that are consistent with those values.

Conclusion

People listened to and followed Jesus, in part, because He was a man of character. People who do what is right in the secret place will also do what is right in the public place. Others will see and be drawn to them. Former professor, author, and educator of educators Findley Edge declared,

> The teacher is like a stained-glass window. The sunshine of God's truth shines through the teacher's mind, spirit, and life. The light takes on the glow and the color of the teacher, whether it be bright and glowing or dark and gloomy (1999, 218).

Jesus was the light of the world. He also says that we are lights (Matt. 5:14). His light filters through the character of our lives. Jerry Self, one of the board members of Heritage Christian University, has served as a schoolteacher, preacher, and elder. In his book *Shepherds*, he expands on the work of McGarvey in his well-known *A Treatise on the Elder-ship*. Having stated that no elder will be perfect in living out the characteristics of elders found in 1 Timothy 3 and Titus 1, brother Self states,

> Every elder should carefully search continually in his own life for these qualities, and any time he finds failure, he should immediately amend his ways, and be sure he is moving in the right direction. It is a fearful thing for someone to be put in a position that places him before others as an example to the church of what a Christian should be like (2017, 81).

Discussion Questions

1. What did you find most helpful or insightful in this lesson?
2. Read Matthew 6:1–8, 16–18 and discuss how this compares to how leaders may act today.
3. What are some ways that leaders may fail to be people of integrity and character?
4. What are some things we can do to help us to be people of integrity?

Homework

1. Satan tempted Jesus as the "Son of God." How would Satan tempt you? Make a mental list of areas in which you would be most vulnerable. How can being aware of these possibilities help you to be a person of integrity?
2. Read through the list of woes in Matthew 23. List modern comparisons to the things highlighted by Jesus.

13

HOW DO YOU DEFINE SUCCESS?

Introduction

MOSES WAS A FAILURE. I hate to be the one to say it, but he was. Just look at his career. He led a generation of Israelites out of Egypt, and only two of the adults made it to the promised land ... two out of a million-plus people. Jeremiah was inept as well. The nation of Judah rejected his preaching and was taken away into captivity in Babylon. Jeremiah himself was kidnapped and taken away to die in Egypt. Numbers do not lie. The numbers say that these so-called great men were failures.

We live in a world of profit margins and standardized testing. We define success by numbers. Kids are rated by whether they score well on an ACT. Who cares if they are the greatest piano player in the history of humanity? Adults are rated by how much money they make or how big their homes are. Who cares if they are decent human beings? Preachers are hired and fired by numbers as well. They are often viewed as too old or too young. They either have too little experience or they have been around too long. I once tried to apply for a preaching position for a congregation in middle Tennessee. I was told they were taking applications only from people over 30 and under 50 years of age. They were hiring "by the numbers." We consider other numbers in determining success. We look at attendance figures, responses, contributions, Sunday night participation, and how long the sermons are. Who cares if the preacher is a man of truth, honesty, and integrity who gives his all to the Lord and his work? Who cares if people are being shaped into the image of Christ? One of my pet peeves has been how people will walk up to you at a conference, workshop, or lectureship and ask, "How big is your congregation?" or "How big is your youth group?" We judge by the numbers.

If Moses or Jeremiah brought their résumés to the average congregation today, could they get a job? Moses would be considered too old and Jeremiah too emotional and inexperienced. If one uses the world's measurements, then God Himself is a failure. His children went astray as well. The problem is not with Moses, Jeremiah, or God. The problem is with our definition of success. A glance at the results of Jesus's leadership and teaching may challenge our definition of what true success is.

The Christ

My claim in this book has been that Jesus is the greatest leader to ever live on this earth. He was centered, capable, connected, compassionate, common, clear-thinking, a coach, and a man of character. One would think that such a leader would have unlimited success. That was not the case—at least it was not the case if you define success by numbers, or at least the initial numbers. Let us consider the reality, the reasons, and the resilience as we ponder the outcome of His leadership.

Reality

John 6 finds Jesus teaching around the Sea of Galilee. The text says, "And a large crowd was following him, because they saw the signs that he was doing on the sick" (John 6:2). Jesus was hugely popular. This popularity would only increase. The verses that follow tell us that Jesus fed five thousand men, not counting women and children, with five loaves and two fishes. The people responded by saying, "This is indeed the Prophet who is to come into the world!" (John 6:14). Based on comments that are made later in John 6, the people were probably alluding to the "prophet like Moses" who is referred to in Deuteronomy 18:17–19. Jesus was so popular that the people got in their boats the next day and crossed the lake to find Him. This sure does sound like Jesus is a "successful" leader!

Unfortunately, by the end of the John 6 people were leaving Him in droves. "After this many of his disciples turned back and no longer walked with him" (John 6:66). This departure was so complete that Jesus asked His apostles, "Do you want to go away as well?" (John 6:67). The way He worded the question in Greek implies He expected them to say, "No" (cf. Rogers and Rogers 1998, 198). This does not change the fact that people were leaving in large numbers and Jesus felt the need to ask His apostles about their commitments. The situation does not get better. Remember that the story of Jesus's ministry culminates at a Roman cross on a hill called Calvary. I guess Jesus was not a success after all.

Reasons

What happened? How could the master teacher end up being rejected and crucified? There were a couple of key reasons for this. First of all, He was working with human beings. There is not a righteous human being, no not one (cf. Rom. 3:10). Humans are weak, frail, and prone to self-centeredness. John 6 identifies some reasons why the people rejected His teaching:

1. They had improper motives (John 6:26–27). They came to see what they could get out of Jesus.
2. They had an improper focus (John 6:27). They were focused on the physical, not the spiritual.
3. They had improper notions of the Messiah (John 6:30–36). They expected a prophet who would feed them physical food as Moses had in the wilderness. Jesus offered them more. He offered them spiritual food. He offered Himself as the bread of life.
4. Jesus's words were difficult to accept (John 6:60). It required a paradigm shift or a change in their view of the world and especially the Messiah. They could not get beyond their preconceived notions to understand Jesus's message.

5. Some just simply refused to believe and change (John 6:61–65).

The second main reason they rejected His teaching is that He had a different goal. He had a different definition of success. In the book *7 Practices of Effective Ministry*, Andy Stanley, Reggie Joiner, and Lane Jones identify "Clarify the Win" as the first practice (2004, 69). "Clarifying the win simply means communicating to your team what is really important and what really matters" (Stanley, Joiner, and Jones 2004, 71). It is determining what qualifies as a win or a success. The authors go on to say,

> Too many church leaders have bought into the myth that to clarify the win means establishing attendance goals and raising a lot of money. These can certainly be indicators about the health of your organization, but strong numbers in these areas do not necessarily mean you are winning (Stanley, Joiner, and Jones 2004, 71).

Jesus did not define success in terms of numbers. This can be seen in how Jesus began the sermon in John 6. The people had traveled across the lake to see Him. Jesus responded by saying, in essence, "You just came for the food" (my loose translation of John 6:26). There are times when Jesus seemed to be trying to run people off. He told one man to go and sell everything he had, and then he could travel with Him (Mark 10:17–22). He told another man who offered to follow Him, "Foxes have holes, and birds of the air have nests, but the Son of Man has nowhere to lay his head" (Matt. 8:20). On yet another occasion He said,

Whoever loves father or mother more than me is not worthy of me, and whoever loves son or daughter more than me is not worthy of me. And whoever does not take his cross and follow me is not worthy of me. Whoever finds his life will lose it, and whoever loses his life for my sake will find it (Matt. 10:37–39).

Didn't Jesus read Dale Carnegie's book about *How to Win Friends and Influence People?* (Does anyone know that book anymore?)

Jesus responded this way because He did not define success using numbers. He had a different set of goals. He came to change hearts and lives. Mere lip service was not a part of His mission or His definition of success. There are many ways to fill church buildings. Some of the ways are godly, and some are ungodly. It is possible to have buildings filled with people who are nothing more than unchanged curiosity seekers (like we see in John 6). They are just as focused on the physical as the day they first walked in the door. It is also possible to have a congregation of only ten members who have been transformed into the image of Christ and are authentically living out God's mission in the world.

Jesus focused on doing the Lord's work and letting God handle the responses. Listen to Jesus's comments in chapter four of John:

Jesus said to them, "*My food is to do the will of him who sent me and to accomplish his work.* Do you not say, 'There are yet four months, then comes the harvest'? Look, I tell you, lift up your eyes, and see that the fields are white for harvest. Already the one who reaps is receiving wages and gathering fruit for eternal life, so that sower and reaper may rejoice together. For here the saying holds true, '*One sows and another reaps*.' I sent you to reap that for which you did not labor. Others have labored, and you have entered into their labor" (John 4:34–38, emphasis mine).

Jesus emphasized that He came to finish the work God gave Him to do. That is exactly what He did. That is why He could say, "It is finished" (John 19:30) on the cross, even though many had rejected Him. His ministry was to proclaim and provide salvation (cf. chapter 3 in this book). His apostles had responsibilities for sowing and reaping after His departure. Still, God is the one who must produce the increase. I am reminded of the words of Paul, "I planted, Apollos watered, but God gave the growth. So neither he who plants nor he who waters is anything, but only God who gives the growth" (1 Cor. 3:6–7). There is no New Testament evidence that God overthrows the human will and forces people to accept Christ, but there is the reality that God is involved in the process of conversion. We may not understand every detail about this interplay between human choice and divine will, yet both are clearly biblical (cf. "kick against the goads" in the conversion of Saul, Acts 26:14). The point is that human response does not lie in the responsibility of the leader. It lies in the heart of the student and in the power of God.

Resilience

Jesus went on doing the Father's work in spite of the discouraging departure of many disciples (cf. John 7–8). Jesus continued to teach no matter what opposition or rejection He faced. How was He able to do this? Habit number two in Covey's book *The Seven Habits of Highly Effective People* is "begin with the end in mind." Covey describes this habit as follows:

> To begin with the end in mind means to start with a clear understanding of your destination. It means to know where you're going so that you better understand where you are now and so that the steps you take are always in right direction (1989, 98).

Covey stresses that before climbing a ladder we need to make sure the ladder is leaned against the right wall. He challenges individuals, families, and organizations to have a mission statement which "becomes the criterion by which you measure everything else in your life" (1989, 129). Chapter three was the chapter in this study in which we first began looking at the leadership traits of Jesus. That chapter stressed that Jesus was centered. He had a clear understanding of the mission for His life. He was able to endure setbacks because He had His own mission and His own definition of success. He did not let the world set His agenda or define success for Him. That is what highly effective people and leaders do. Thus, Moses, Jeremiah, and God Himself were not failures after all. It is only our limited definition of success that has failed.

The Christian

Chris McChesney, Sean Covey, and Jim Huling have authored an outstanding book on leadership titled *The 4 Disciplines of Execution*. The second discipline that they discuss is "Act on the Lead Measures." They observe,

> *Lag measures* are the tracking measurements of the wildly important goal, and they are usually the ones you spend most of your time praying over. Revenue, profit, market share, and customer satisfaction are all lag measures, meaning that when you receive them, the performance that drove them is already in the past (McChesney, Covey, and Huling 2012, 11–12).

On the other hand, you have lead measures. *"Lead measures* are quite different in that they are the measures of the most high-impact things your team must do to reach the goal" (McChesney, Covey, and Huling 2012, 12). Lead measures are the action steps that lead to good lag measures. It is about the actions that lead to good numbers. The authors are not saying that the lag measures (the numbers) do not matter. They are simply encouraging executives to focus more attention on the lead measures than the lag measures. What we have seen in this chapter is that the spiritual lag measures are not all in the leaders' control. What we can control are our personal lead measures. We can focus on doing the right things in the right ways that lead to right results. If we focus only on the results, we may become discouraged. If we focus on doing the right things, we will persevere in moving forward with God's work.

Always remember that human beings are fickle. Today

they will sing your praises and lay palm leaves in your path (cf. Matt. 21:8–11), and a week later they will cry out for your crucifixion (cf. Matt. 27:22). If you lead people, they are going to let you down eventually. There will be days when it seems that leading in the Lord's church just is not worth it. Remember five things when those days come. First, we are humans who mess up as well. We can expect no less of others. Second, we need to focus on our job of planting and watering. Our job is to do our job. The results are up to someone else. The third thing to remember is not to buy into the world's definition of success. Success is not determined by numbers. It is better to have one changed heart than to have a hundred curiosity seekers who are focused on self. By the way, do not give up on the curiosity seekers. Some of them may change as well. The fourth principle is not to live for human praise. Leaders who lead for the Lord do not live to be honored by human beings. They live to hear, "Well done, good and faithful servant. You have been faithful over a little; I will set you over much. Enter into the joy of your master" (Matt. 25:21). Finally, do not focus on the short-term results. Jesus left this world 2,000 years ago, yet His name is known around the globe, and in the intervening years millions of people have come to believe in His name. He was mocked while on the cross. Luke 23 tells us that three groups or individuals mocked Jesus as king or Christ (23:35–37, 39). Christ means "anointed one." The Jewish kings of the Old Testament were known as God's anointed (cf. 1 Sam. 24:10). By the first century, the term "Christ" referred to the promised king, the descendant of David, who would rule forever (2 Sam. 7:12–17). They mocked Him as "the King of the Jews" because He looked like anything but a king. But Paul tells us that because Jesus humbled Himself to the point of dying on a cross, "therefore God has highly exalted him and bestowed on him the name that is above every name, so that at the name of Jesus every knee should bow, in heaven and on earth and under the earth, and every tongue confess that Jesus Christ is Lord, to the glory of God the Father" (Phil. 2:9–11). Jesus did not let the cross stop Him from fulfilling His mission. He completed His task (John 19:30), and the rest is history and eternity.

Conclusion

Author and Chicago Sun-Times columnist Sydney J. Harris stated, "A failure is not someone who has tried and failed; it is someone who has given up trying and resigned himself to failure; it is not a condition, but an attitude." (quoted in Manser 2001, 100). I do not want to mislead you. If you choose to lead like Jesus, it will not be easy. If Jesus was unable to convert everyone, then we can expect to have setbacks and discouragement in our leadership walks with God as well. I challenge you to find a place to lead in God's kingdom and to remain faithful to your task. Maybe no one will follow you. Caleb and Joshua stood alone (Num. 14:5–10). No one followed. Sometimes that is what great leaders must do. Lead on anyway. Your life will be a success if in the end you can say, "It is finished. I spent my life faithfully serving the Lord." And who knows, God just may multiply the seeds you planted and change the world.

As our study comes to a close, I am reminded of a scene from the movie *Jurassic Park III*. A group of people was trapped on the dinosaur-infested Costa Rican island of Isla Sorna. They traveled to the island to rescue a young boy,

Eric Kirby, who was stranded there as the result of a paragliding accident. There is a scene in which Dr. Alan Grant's young friend and protégé, Billy Brennan, had just been carried away by a giant pterodactyl. In the aftermath, a reflective Dr. Grant, a paleontologist, described his friend to Eric. He stated, "I have a theory that there are two kinds of boys: There are those who want to be astronomers and those who want to be astronauts. The astronomer, the pale-ontologist, gets to study these amazing things from a place of complete safety." Eric then responds, "But then you never get to go into space." Dr. Grant goes on to say that Billy had the astronaut's perspective (*Jurassic Park III* 2001). This is a powerful analogy. Astronomers study the stars. Astronauts fly toward them. Which will you be? Will you be a leadership astronomer or a leadership astronaut? Will you just study and read about leadership or will you go and be a leader, and in the process take people to places they never would have gone, destinations set in the will of the Creator of all the universe? Do not just read, reach for the stars. Go change the world. Make a difference. Lead like the Lord for the Lord!

Discussion Questions

1. What did you find most helpful in this lesson?
2. Discuss how we should define success for spiritual leaders.
3. Read Numbers 14:5–10. Some believe that a person is not a leader if there are no followers. Discuss whether you agree or disagree with this and why.

Homework

1. Read through John 6 and list five things that stand out to you.
2. Read Luke 23:32–43. Discuss how the people's understanding of the job of the Christ differed from Jesus's true mission.

Bibliography

à Kempis, Thomas. 1958. *The Imitation of Christ*. Chicago: Moody.

Bagents, Bill, and Rosemary Snodgrass. 2021. *Counseling for Church Leaders*. Florence, AL: Cypress Publications.

Band of Brothers. 2001. New York: HBO.

Banks, Robert, and Bernice M. Ledbetter. 2004. *Reviewing Leadership: A Christian Evaluation of Current Approaches*. Grand Rapids: Baker Academic.

Barber, Jerrie. 2015. "Appointing New Elders." Pages 86–97 in *Rest in Green Pastures: Encouragement for Shepherds*. Edited by Chris McCurley. Dallas: Start2Finish.

Barna, George, ed. 1997. *Leaders on Leadership: Wisdom, Advice and Encouragement on the Art of Leading God's People*. Ventura, CA: Regal.

Bennis, Warren, and Burt Nanus. 1985. *Leaders: Strategies for Taking Charge*. New York: Harper & Row.

Black, Wesley. 2008. "Stopping the Dropouts: Guiding Adolescents Toward a Lasting Faith Following High School Graduation." *Christian Education Journal* 3.5: 28–46.

Blackaby, Henry, and Richard Blackaby. 2001. *Spiritual Leadership: Moving People on to God's Agenda*. Nashville: Broadman & Holman.

_____. 2011. *Spiritual Leadership: Moving People on to God's Agenda*. Rev. and exp. ed. Nashville: Broadman & Holman.

Bolsinger, Tod. 2015. *Canoeing the Mountains: Christian Leadership in Uncharted Territory*. Exp. ed. Downers Grove, IL: InterVarsity Press.

Braddy, Ken. 2017. "Discipling in an Age of Biblical Illiteracy," *Lifeway Research*.
    https://lifewayresearch.com/2017/07/10/disciplingin-an-age-of-biblical-illiteracy/.

Brooks, Phillips. 1950. *Phillips Brooks: Selected Sermons*. Edited by William Scarlett. New York: Dutton & Company.

Brothers, Kirk. 2010. "A Cross-Cultural Study of Factors Motivating Church of Christ Ministry Students to Enter Ministry." PhD diss., The Southern Baptist Theological Seminary.

_____. 2014. "The Preacher and Sin." Pages 91–102 in *Fit for the Pulpit*. Edited by Chris McCurley. Bowie, TX: Start2Finish.

Byron, George Gordon. 1882. *Hours of Idleness: A Series of Poems, Original and Translated*. Paris: Galignani.

Carnegie, Dale. 1936. *How to Win Friends and Influence People*. New York: Simon & Schuster.

Cohen, Jack, and Ian Stewart. 1994. *The Collapse of Chaos: Discovering Simplicity in a Complex World*. New York: Viking.

Cohen, William. 2010. *Heroic Leadership: Leading with Integrity and Honor*. San Francisco: Jossey-Bass.

Collins, Jim. 2001. *Good to Great: Why Some Companies Make the Leap… and Others Don't*. New York: Collins.

Covey, Stephen R. 1989. *The Seven Habits of Highly Effective People: Powerful Lessons in Personal Change*. New York: Simon & Schuster.

Cox, James D. 1976. *With the Bishops and Deacons*. Delight, AR: Gospel Light Publishing.

Danker, Fredrick W. 2000. *A Greek-English Lexicon of the New Testament and Other Early Christian Literature*. 3rd ed. Chicago: University of Chicago Press.

De Pree, Max. 2004. *Leadership Is an Art*. New York: Currency.

Dillinger, Jeffrey. 1996. "The Man of Compassion." Pages 101–105 in *Man of God: Essays on the Life and Work of the Preacher*. Edited by Shawn D. Mathis. Nashville: Gospel Advocate.

Drucker, Peter F. 1974. *Management: Tasks, Responsibilities, Practices*. New York: Harper & Row.

_____. 1990. *Managing the Nonprofit Organization: Principles and Practices*. New York: Harper.

Edge, Findley B. 1999. *Teaching for Results*. Rev. ed. Nashville: Broadman & Holman.

Edmondson, Michael. 2020. *Navigate the Chaos in 2020*. Michael Edmondson.

Estep, James, Jr. 2005. "Decision Making and Communication within the Organization." Pages 222–239 in *Management Essentials for Christian Ministries*. Edited by Michael J. Anthony and James Estep, Jr. Nashville: Broadman & Holman.

Fair, Ian A. 2008. *Leadership in the Kingdom: Sensitive Strategies for the Church in a Changing World*. Abilene, TX: ACU Press.

Farrar, Steve. 1990. *Point Man: How a Man Can Lead His Family*. Colorado Springs: Multnomah.

Fisher, David. 1996. *The 21st Century Pastor: A Vision Based on the Ministry of Paul*. Grand Rapids: Zondervan.

Gangel, Kenneth O. 1997. *Team Leadership in Christian Ministry: Using Multiple Gifts to Build a Unified Vision*. Chicago: Moody.

Geiger, Eric, and Kevin Peck. 2016. *Designed to Lead: The Church and Leadership Development*. Nashville: Broadman & Holman.

Gospel of John, The. 2003. Nashville: Visual Bible International.

Groom, Winston. 2015. *The Generals: Patton, MacArthur, Marshall, and the Winning of World War II*. Read by Robertson Dean. Ashland, OR: Blackstone Audio. Audio edition.

Gross, Anthony. 1912. *Lincoln's Own Stories*. Garden City, NY: Harper & Brothers.

Hagner, Donald A. 1993. *Matthew 1–13*. WBC 33A. Dallas: Word.

Holland, Thomas H. 2000. *Sermon Design and Delivery*. 2nd ed. Brentwood, TN: Penmann.

Johnson, Aubrey. 2014. *Dynamic Deacons: Champions of Christ's Church*. Sharpsburg, GA: Aubrey Johnson Ministries.

_____. 2019. *Successful Shepherds: Leading People in Paths of Righteousness*. Lebanon, TN: Aubrey Johnson Ministries. Kindle edition.

Jurassic Park III. 2001. Orlando: Universal Studios.

Keener, Craig S. 1993. *The IVP Bible Background Commentary: New Testament*. Downers Grove, IL: InterVarsity Press.

King, Martin Luther, Jr. 1984. *Strength to Love*. Large print ed. New York: Walker & Company.

Kittel, Gerhard, and Gerhard Friedrich, eds. 1972. *Theological Dictionary of the New Testament*. Translated by Geoffrey W. Bromiley. Volume VIII. Grand Rapids: Eerdmans.

Kouzes, James M., and Barry Z. Posner, eds. 2004. *Christian Reflections on the Leadership Challenge*. San Francisco: Wiley & Sons.

_____. 2017. *The Leadership Challenge: How to Make Extraordinary Things Happen in Organizations*. 6th ed. Hoboken, NJ: Wiley & Sons.

Lencioni, Patrick. 2002. *The Five Dysfunctions of a Team: A Leadership Fable*. San Francisco: Jossey-Bass.

Lomenick, Brad. 2015. *H3 Leadership: Be Humble, Stay Hungry, Always Hustle*. Nashville: Nelson.

Louw, Johannes P., and Eugene A. Nida, eds. 1989. *Greek-English Lexicon of the New Testament Based on Semantic Domains*. Volume 1. 2nd ed. New York: United Bible Societies.

MacArthur, John. 2002. *Twelve Ordinary Men: How the Master Shaped His Disciples for Greatness, and What He Wants to Do with You*. Nashville: Nelson.

_____. 2004. *Called to Lead: 26 Leadership Lessons from the Life of the Apostle Paul.* Nashville: Nelson.

Manser, Martin H., Comp. 2001. *The Westminster Collection of Christian Quotations: Over 6000 Quotations Arranged by Theme.* Louisville: Westminster John Knox.

Maxwell, John C. 1995. *Developing the Leaders Around You: How to Help Others Reach Their Full Potential.* Nashville: Nelson.

_____. 2003. *Equipping 101: What Every Leader Needs to Know.* Nashville: Nelson.

_____. 2003. *Relationships 101: What Every Leader Needs to Know.* Nashville: Nelson.

_____. 2004. *Winning with People: Discover the People Principles That Work for You Every Time.* Nashville: Nelson.

Maxwell, John C., and Tim Elmore, eds. 2007. *The Maxwell Leadership Bible.* New King James Version. 2nd ed. Nashville: Nelson.

McChesney, Chris, Sean Covey, and Jim Huling. 2012. *The 4 Disciplines of Execution: Achieving Your Wildly Important Goals.* New York: Free Press.

McCord, Hugo. 1996. "Jesus As an Example for Preachers." Pages 23–28 in *Man of God: Essays on the Life and Work of the Preacher.* Edited by Shawn D. Mathis. Nashville: Gospel Advocate.

McGarvey, J. W. 2010. *A Treatise on the Eldership*. Chillicothe, OH: DeWard.

McLellan, Vern. 2000. *Wise Words and Quotes*. Wheaton, IL: Tyndale House.

Meeks, Janet Smith. 2017. *Gracious Leadership: Lead Like You've Never Led Before*. Westlake, OH: Smart Business Network.

Metaxas, Eric. 2015. *7 Men and the Secret of Their Greatness*. Nashville: Nelson.

Mitchell, Stan. 2010. *Equipping the Saints for the Ministry*. Henderson, TN: Hester Publications.

Mohler, Albert. 2012. *The Conviction to Lead: 25 Principles for Leadership That Matters*. Bloomington, MN: Bethany House.

_____. 2016. "The Scandal of Biblical Illiteracy: It's Our Problem."
   https://albertmohler.com/2016/01/20/the-scandal-of-biblical-illiteracy-its-our-problem-4.

Mounce, William D., ed. 2006. *Mounce's Complete Expository Dictionary of Old and New Testament Words*. Grand Rapids: Zondervan.

Ogden, Greg, and Daniel Meyer. 2007. *Leadership Essentials: Shaping Vision, Multiplying Influence, Defining Character*. Downers Grove, IL: IVP Connect.

Pells, Eddie. 2016. "Golden rule: For US relays, holding onto baton is job No.1," *AP*. https://apnews.com/article/ae5a136ad36044e1b7b48 b6f19ca77f5.

Powell, Kara, Jake Mulder, and Brad Griffin. 2016. *Growing Young: 6 Essential Strategies to Help Young People Discover and Love Your Church*. Grand Rapids: Baker.

Price, J. M. 1985. *Jesus the Teacher*. Rev. ed. Nashville: Convention Press.

Richards, Lawrence O., and Gary J. Bredfeldt. 1998. *Creative Bible Teaching*. Rev. and exp. ed. Chicago: Moody.

Rogers, Cleon L. Jr., and Cleon L. Rogers III. 1998. *The New Linguistic and Exegetical Key to the Greek New Testament*. Grand Rapids: Zondervan.

Rost, Joseph C. 1993. *Leadership for the Twenty-First Century*. Westport, CT: Praeger.

Seeley, Thomas D. 2010. *Honeybee Democracy*. Princeton: Princeton University Press.

Self, Jerry. 2017. *Shepherds: Leaders in the Church*. Charleston, SC: Jerry Self.

Simpson, Alan K. 1999. Introduction to Gerald R. Ford's speech delivered at Harvard University's Kennedy School of Government's ARCO Forum. Cambridge, MA, 17 March.

Sinek, Simon. 2017. *Leaders Eat Last: Why Some Teams Pull Together and Others Don't*. New York: Portfolio.

Sloan, Robert B. 2011. "A Biblical Model of Leadership." Pages 8–23 in *Christian Leadership Essentials: A Handbook for Managing Christian Organizations*. Edited by David S. Dockery. Nashville: Broadman & Holman.

Smith, Christian. 2005. *Soul Searching: The Religious and Spiritual Lives of American Teenagers*. Oxford: Oxford University Press.

Smith, Gordon T. 2017. *Institutional Intelligence: How to Build an Effective Organization*. Downers Grove, IL: InterVarsity Press.

Stanley, Andy. 2016. *Visioneering: Your Guide for Discovering and Maintaining Personal Vision*. Colorado Springs: Multnomah.

Stanley, Andy, Reggie Joiner, and Lane Jones. 2004. *7 Practices of Effective Ministry*. Sisters, OR: Multnomah.

Stott, John R. W. 1982. *Between Two Worlds: The Art of Preaching in the Twentieth Century*. Grand Rapids: Eerdmans.

Thayer, Joseph Henry. 1886. *A Greek-English Lexicon of the New Testament*. Corrected ed. New York: American Book Company.

Tichy, Noel M., with Nancy Cardwell. 2002. *The Cycle of Leadership: How Great Leaders Teach Their Companies to Win*. New York: HarperBusiness.

Tierney, Thomas J. 2006. "Understanding the Nonprofit Sector's Leadership Deficit." Pages 95–105 in *The Leader of the Future 2: Visions, Strategies, and Practices for the New Era.* Edited by Frances Hesselbein and Marshall Goldsmith. San Francisco: Jossey-Bass.

Turner, Bob. 2020. *Essential: Building Blocks 4 Life and Leadership.* Columbia, SC: Bob Turner.

Turner, J. J. 2005. *Shepherds, Wake Up!: Ancient Training for Modern Shepherds.* Huntsville, AL: Publishing Designs.

_____. 2013. *Leading by the Book: Biblical Leadership Principles.* Scotts Valley, CA: CreateSpace.

"Two Ducks and a Frog." 1989. *Today in the Word* 4:34.

Whitney, Donald S. 1991. *Spiritual Disciplines for the Christian Life.* Colorado Springs: NavPress.

Wilder, Michael S., and Timothy Paul Jones. 2018. *The God Who Goes Before You: Pastoral Leadership as Christ-Centered Fellowship.* Nashville: B & H Academic.

Willard, Dallas. 1997. *The Divine Conspiracy: Rediscovering Our Hidden Life in God.* San Francisco: HarperSanFrancisco.

Wilson, Marlene. 2004. *Volunteer Job Descriptions and Action Plans.* Loveland, CO: Group.

_____. 2004. *Volunteer Orientation and Training.* Loveland, CO: Group.

Webster's Third New International Dictionary. 2002. Edited by Philip Babcock Gove. Springfield, MA: Merriam-Webster.

Work, Mike, and Ginny Olson. 2014. *Youth Ministry Management Tools 2.0: Everything You Need to Successfully Manage Your Ministry*. Grand Rapids: Zondervan.

Yeakley, Flavil R., Jr. 2014. *Shepherding God's Flock*. Nashville: 21st Century Christian.

Zenger, John H., and Joseph Folkman. 2002. *The Extraordinary Leader: Turning Good Managers into Great Leaders*. New York: McGraw-Hill.

Modern Name Index

Scripture Index

About the Author

W. Kirk Brothers is the president of Heritage Christian University. Dr. Brothers spent twenty-three years in local ministry before transitioning to a more formal teaching role in 2010. He was a professor at Freed-Hardeman University for eight years before becoming the president of HCU in 2018. He also teaches a course at the Bible School of the Americas in Panama and implements Future Minister Training camps for young men throughout Latin America and South America. He is married to Cindy. They have two daughters, Katie and Hannah.

Also by Heritage Christian University
Press in Cooperation with Heritage
Christian Leadership Institute

Counseling for Church Leaders
by Bill Bagents and Rosemary Snodgrass